MW00851869

FALLSCHIRM-JÄGER RGT. 3

A PICTORIAL HISTORY

Volume 1: From Storm Battalion
to Regiment 1916/1941

EINE CHRONIK IN BILDERN

Band 1: Vom Sturmbataillon
zum Regiment 1916/1941

K L A U S   J.   P E T E R S

1st EDITION

Copyright 1992 by Klaus J. Peters
ISBN No. 0-912138-46-7
Designed by Roger James Bender
Published by R. James Bender Publ.,
P.O. Box 23456, San Jose, CA 95153
Printed in the United States of America

TABLE OF CONTENTS

INHALTSVERZEICHNIS

FOREWORD
by
Prof. Dr. Freiherr von der Heydte, General (Rtd.)

VORWORT
von
Prof. Dr. Freiherr von der Heydte, General d. Res. a.D.

Commencing in 1914, artillery observers in captive balloons carried the newly-developed parachute as an "aerial life-preserver" in the event that they were shot down. By 1917, German military pilots and aircrews were also equipped with parachutes which at least gave them a fighting chance for survival if their aircraft were shot down. It was logical, therefore, for the military to consider the use of parachutes to drop combat troops behind enemy lines. In point of fact, this was done by the French on the Western Front and by the Germans on the Eastern Front. In 1918, U.S. General Billy Mitchell considered the idea of dropping an entire U.S. infantry division behind German lines but this revolutionary tactic was never executed due to the German surrender in November of that year.

In 1925, the Red Army commenced the use of parachute units for military missions. The German Reichswehr profited from these early foreign experimentations, being exposed to the airborne concept while their clandestine pilots and aircrews were secretly trained at the Russian airfield of Lipzek.

Schon seit Anfang des 1. Weltkrieges diente der Fallschirm den Artilleriebeobachtern in Fesselballons als "Rettungsring der Lüfte," um im Falle des Abschusses sicher zur Erde zurückzukehren. Deutsche Piloten und Flugzeugbesatzungen wurden erst Anfang 1917 mit Fallschirmen ausgerüstet, wodurch sich die Chance, bei einem Abschuss zu überleben, wesentlich verbesserte. Der Gedanke, den Fallschirm auch dazu zu nutzen, um Soldaten aus Flugzeugen hinter den feindlichen Linien abzusetzen, lag also sehr nahe und wurde schon vereinzelt während des 1. Weltkrieges praktiziert. Ende 1918 griff der amerikanische General Mitchell diesen Gedanken auf, jedoch konnte seine Absicht, eine ganze Division hinter den deutschen Linien per Fallschirm landen zu lassen, durch die Kapitulation nicht mehr verwirklicht werden.

Etwa ab 1925 wurden in der Sowjetunion weiterführende Versuche unternommen, um den Fallschirm militärisch zu nutzen. Von diesen Versuchen profitierte auch die deutsche Reichswehr, die mit Duldung der politischen Führung unter strengster Geheimhaltung auf dem russischen Flugplatz Lipzek

After January 31, 1927, following the departure of the Allied Control Commission from Germany, the Reichswehr pursued their development and expansion of airborne training on their own territory.

With the rebirth of the Luftwaffe in 1935, the new Minister for Air, Hermann Göring gathered all airforce units, including the fledgling airborne troops, under his control. He intended to expand his new airborne infantry force by training Prussian Police personnel, then under his control as Minister-President of Prussia, as parachute troops. Unfortunately, this concept failed because the well-motivated police officers had no concept of recent developments in military thinking in general, or airborne tactics in particular.

In September of 1935, Reichswehr Major Kurt Student was assigned by Göring to develop and expand the concept of airborne operations within the Luftwaffe. Student was a well-known World War I fighter pilot, and when he commenced working on the development of the parachute troops as head of the new Luftwaffe technical school, he at once realized the potential of this new branch for combat behind the lines of an enemy. He did not embrace the

---

den Grundstock für ihre zukünftige Luftwaffe legte. Hier wurden Piloten ausgebildet, Luftfahrtgeräte getestet und Spezialisten weitergebildet. Nachdem am 31.Januar 1927 die alliierte Kontrollkommission abzog, war es möglich, auch in Deutschland mit dem Luftgerät Fallschirm zu experimentieren. Nach der Wiedergeburt der deutschen Luftwaffe beanspruchte Göring auch den Oberbefehl über die in Entstehung begriffene deutsche Fallschirmtruppe. Da er preussischer Ministerpräsident und damit Oberbefehlshaber der preussischen, kasernierten Polizei war, griff er beim Aufbau des Führungskaders zunächst auf die Offiziere der ihm unterstellten Polizei zurück. Obgleich diese Offiziere persönlich sehr trainiert und einsatzwillig waren, fehlten ihnen die taktische Schulung im Kampf der verbundenen Waffen und die besonderen Kenntnisse im Luftlandeeinsatz.

Den damaligen Reichswehr-Major Student, der schon im 1. Weltkrieg als Pilot sich einen Namen verschafft hatte und als Kommandeur der technischen Schule der zukünftigen Luftwaffe vorgesehen war, betraute Göring mit dem

idea of using parachutists as small "special forces" who would conduct reconnaissance in force and attack limited military objectives, but saw their role as instruments of strategic warfare and as a spearhead for advancing army ground units.

It was also his wish that all airborne forces should be under the single command of the Luftwaffe. In this, he was strongly supported by the politically powerful Göring and so the Army Airborne Infantry Battalion, the only such unit not under Luftwaffe control, came under Göring's command in January of 1939.

The initial combat experience of this new force in the Polish campaign of 1939 and the Norwegian campaign of 1940 quickly demonstrated the dangerous lack of tactical knowledge on the part of the former Prussian Police cadre. Göring, therefore, decided to raise another parachute regiment using a cadre from the old Army Airborne Infantry Battalion.

Following the conclusion of the campaign in the West, Colonel Richard Heidrich, an experienced infantry officer and former tactical instructor, initiated the raising of the new Parachute Regiment 3 at Bergen. Heidrich gave his soldiers proper combat training, developed an excellent "esprit de corps," and insisted that all his officers acquire a complete understanding of all phases of infantry and airborne warfare. If an officer was unable to do so, Heidrich required his transfer.

Aufbau, der Ausbildung und der Führung der neu zu schaffenden Fallschirmtruppe. Student erkannte in dieser neuen Truppengattung den operativen.Wert, den der geschlossene Einsatz von kampfkräftigen Verbänden in der "vertikalen Umfassung" für das Heer haben könnte. Er sah Fallschirmjäger nicht in der Rolle der Späh- und Zerstörtrupps, die allein auf sich gestellt oder im kleinen Rahmen hinter den feidlichen Linien operieren sollten. Student erkannte aber auch, dass Fallschirmeinheiten unter einem Kommando und unter einheitlicher Führung durch die Luftwaffe stehen sollten. So wurde am 01.01.1939 das Fallschirminfanterie-Bataillon des Heeres als II. Bataillon des Fallschirmjägerregiment 1 in die Luftwaffe übernommen.

Die ersten Kriegseinsätze in Polen und Norwegen zeigten den Mangel der taktischen Schulung der aus der Polizei hervorgegangenen Unterführer und Führer. Deshalb schlug er Göring noch vor dem Frankreichfeldzug die Aufstellung eines dritten Fallschirmjägerregimentes vor, dessen Führer und Unterführer in ihrer grossen Mehrheit sich aus den im Hunderttausend-Mann-Heer gut ausgebildeten Offizieren und Unteroffizieren des Heeres zusammensetzen sollte. Nach Ende des Frankreichfeldzuges wurde dieses Fallschirmjägerregiment 3 unter Führung des bereits im Fallschirmeinsatz erfahrenen und als Taktiklehrer bestens bewährten Oberst Richard Heidrich aufgestellt.

Heidrich verstand es, seine Fallschirmjäger zu einer Elite auszubilden, den Zusammenhalt mit den Familien zu erhalten und gleichzeitig den Korpsgeist im Regiment zu pflegen. Dem Offizierkorps des Fallschirmjägerregimentes 3 anzugehören galt als Auszeichnung; Offiziere, die den Anforderungen

Parachute Regiment 3 was to become one of the most successful units of the Wehrmacht, for wherever and whenever it received the order to fight, be it on Crete or Sicily, in Russia or Italy, it did so with honors, courage and with much success.

Frhr. v. d. Heydte

Heidrichs nicht genügten, wurden von ihm rücksichtslos zur Versetzung in ein anderes Fallschirmjägerregiment vorgeschlagen. Dieser besonders guten, taktischen Schulung des Offizier- und Unteroffizierkorps ist es sicher zu verdanken, dass das Fallschirmjägerregiment 3 sich im Laufe des 2. Weltkrieges besonders bewährte und stets alle Aufträge mit grossem Erfolg erfüllte.

Frhr. v. d. Heydte

Frhr.
v.d. Heydte.

INTRODUCTION

EINFÜHRUNG

One can still tour the preserved portions of the World War I battlefields on the Western Front and envisage the destructive savagry of trench warfare. Whole areas of France were reduced to moonscape-like rubble and for years, nothing would grow where the great, lumbering and entrenched armies of the first worldwide conflict bled to death.

The destruction of the second great world war was directed more against the civilian populations and most of the cities and factories have been rebuilt. Unlike the carefully preserved sections of the 1914-1918 battlefields, little remains of the ruins and rubble in the German civilian centers.

Wars, once the games of kings and princes, have long ceased to be the occupation of gentlemen and have passed into the hands of professional politicians and scientists with terrifying results. There are very few who would find themselves opposed to the statement that there never was a good war or a bad peace.

This book shows photographically, the history of two elite German units during both of the world wars. Each unit represents an expression of creativity

Noch heute geben die Schlachtfelder in Belgien und Frankreich Zeugnis von dem unvorstellbaren Ausmass der Materialschlachten und Grabenkämpfe des 1. Weltkrieges. Noch immer werden die Besucher der Mahnmale Verdun und Douamont beeindruckt von der Grausamkeit des Krieges. Trotz dieser Spuren ist der 1. Weltkrieg für die beteiligten Nationen abgeschlossen und zur Geschichte geworden.

Auch der 2. Weltkrieg hat seine Spuren in Europa sichtbar hinterlassen. Schlachtfelder und zahllose Soldatenfriedhöfe sind noch heute überall zu finden. Wenngleich auch der 2. Weltkrieg schon in die Geschichtsbücher eingegangen ist, politisch ist er noch nicht ganz abgeschlossen. Die Auswirkungen dieses verhängnisvollen Krieges beeinflussen noch heute die politischen Ereignisse und Entwicklungen. Vor allem eine Lehre müsste aus der europäischen Vergangenheit dieses Jahrhunderts gezogen werden: Nie wieder dürfen Konflikte zwischen den Völkern mit Waffengewalt gelöst werden! Der Krieg ist nicht mehr "die Fortsetzung der Politik mit anderen Mitteln." Wenn die Menschen von heute und morgen diese Lehre ziehen und sie

born of military necessity and shows very clearly how tactics evolve. It is not written in any sense as a complete unit history but is an attempt to sketch out and document this evolution in the organization, training and battles fought by these emerging elites.

This in-depth photo study is possible only because a few former German paratroopers, Hans Mordhorst and Jakob Stephani, set out to establish a photographic record of their unit shortly after the end of the war in 1945. Through their efforts they were not only successful in determining the fates of numerous MIAs, but also laid the groundwork for this pictorial history of German airborne infantry in general and Parachute Regiment 3 in specific.

This first volume traces the traditions of the army airborne infantry, commencing in 1916 with the establishment of Assault Battalion 7 and works through the organization of the army paratroopers to conclude with the establishment of Parachute Regiment 3 in 1940.

The second volume will be concerned with the combat history of this unit from 1941 to 1945, based on many photographs as well as combat reports, war diaries, casualty lists and so on.

Many former members of Parachute Regiment 3 have been instrumental in the production of this first volume, and thanks are given here to all of them as well as the Associations for the Parachute Infantry Company, Parachute Infantry Battalion and Parachute Regiment 3.

---

als Richtlinie ihrer Politik machen, dann wären zumindest die vielen Soldaten und Opfer des 1. und 2. Weltkrieges nicht umsonst gestorben!

Dieses Buch will mit Bildern den Leidensweg zweier deutscher Eliteverbände in zwei Weltkriegen aufzeigen und darstellen. Es ist keine Chronik im Sinne einer militär-historischen Dokumentation, vielmehr nur der Versuch, mit Bildern den chronologischen Ablauf von Aufstellung, Ausbildung, Einsatz und Kampf nachzuvollziehen und die Bilder für sich sprechen zu lassen. Dass diese Bildgeschichte überhaupt zusammengestellt werden konnte, ist dem glücklichen Umstand zu verdanken, dass schon kurz nach Ende des 2. Weltkrieges einige Überlebende des Fallschirmjägerregiments 3 daran gingen, Vermisstenschicksale nachzuforschen und aufzuklären. Dieser schweren und uneigennützigen Sache stellten sich Herr Hans Mordhorst und Jakob Stephani. Sie sammelten Bilder des Regimentes und befragten dabei die ehemaligen Kameraden und Überlebenden. Ihrer mühevollen Arbeit ist es zu verdanken, dass nicht nur viele ungewisse Schicksale von Vermissten geklärt werden konnten, sondern dass ihre Bildsammlung die Grundlage zur Darstellung der Bildgeschichte der Fallschirminfanterie und des Fallschirmjägerregiments 3 wurde.

Der vorliegende erste Bildteil, der den Zeitraum von 1916 bis 1941 abdeckt und das Entstehen der Fallschirminfanterie der Wehrmacht bis zur Aufstellung des Luftwaffen-Fallschirmjägerregiments 3 darstellt, wird noch ergänzt werden durch die Bildchronik der Kriegseinsätze. Wenngleich dadurch eine Art Bildchronik entstanden ist, müsste dieses Werk noch durch eine tiefergehende Regimentsgeschichte mit Auszügen aus den

In addition, special recognition is also given to Bundesarchiv Koblenz, Bildarchiv des Bundes Deutscher Fallschirmjäger, and:

K. Büttner	K.-W. Mogge
S. Cook	Dr. E. Neumann
R. Donth	G. Petersen
G. Douglas	M. Pöppel
F. Einberger	F. Rentzsch
K. Esche	W. Rohrbach
A. Ex	K. Schrader
H. Gabbey	P. Stahl
F. Glössner	F. Stangenberg
O. Heckel	J. Stephani
Frh. v.d. Heydte	F. Thaler
S. Jamrowski	C. Tietjen
H. Klare	K. Veth
R. Klein	M. Voit
G. Knacke	R. Witzig
A. Ludwig	J. Wüstner
H. Meyer	G. Zimmermann

Kriegstagebüchern, Gefechtsberichten, Aufzeichnungen, Stellenbesetzungen usw. ergänzt werden. Nur so wäre die Gesamtdarstellung der Fallschirminfanterie und des FJR 3 in sich geschlossen und eine wichtige Quelle.

Der erste Teil der Bildchronik, basierend auf der Bildersammlung H. Mordhorst, wurde von vielen ehemaligen Fallschirmjägern der Traditionsgemeinschaft FJR 3 und ehem. F.I.K.-F.I.B. tatkräftig unterstützt. Ihnen allen gilt mein herzlicher Dank!

Ganz besonders zu danken have ich allerdings dem Bundesarchiv Koblenz, dem Bildarchiv des Bundes Deutscher Fallschirmjäger und den Herren:

K. Büttner	A. Ludwig	M. Voit
S. Cook	H. Meyer	R. Witzig
R. Donth	K.-W. Mogge	J. Wüstner
G. Douglas	Dr. E. Neumann	G. Zimmermann
F. Einberger	G. Petersen	
K. Esche	M. Pöppel	
A. Ex	F. Rentzsch	
H. Gabbey	W. Rohrbach	
F. Glössner	K. Schrader	
O. Heckel	P. Stahl	
Frh. v.d. Heydte	F. Stangenberg	
S. Jamrowski	J. Stephani	
H. Klare	F. Thaler	
R. Klein	C. Tietjen	
G. Knacke	K. Veth	

Ohne ihre Hilfe wäre der erste Teil der Bildchronik nicht entstanden!

ASSAULT BATTALION No. 7
Assault Grenadiers - Tactics and Techniques of a new Elite

DAS STURMBATAILLON Nr. 7
Sturmgrenadiere - Taktik und Technik einer neuen Elite

By November of 1914, the Western Front stretched from the North Sea to the Swiss frontier. After initial successes, the German Supreme Command was forced to adopt defensive trench warfare after their reverses in the Battle of the Marne.

The war of attrition began; cavalry and massed infantry charges were replaced with heavy artillery, the machine gun and the entrenching shovel. The infantry entrenched itself deeper and deeper into French soil and the spreading lines of trenches were fortified, wired, mined and barricaded. The ensuing battles in Flanders, the Somme and the great slaughterhouse of Verdun caused massive losses in manpower on both sides with almost no gain of territory on either side. The tactics tried at Verdun, to lure the enemy into a fatal battle of attrition, had failed and the more thoughtful members of the German military leadership cast about for better tactics which could enable a breakthrough of what had proved to be a nearly impregnible front.

The British answer was to develop the tank, while the Germans began to experiment with the use of small, well-equipped and trained assault battalions.

Nach anfänglichen operativen Erfolgen im Westen musste die deutsche Oberste Heeresleitung nach der verlorenen Marneschlacht zum Stellungskrieg übergehen. Die Fronten reichten im November 1914 von der Nordsee bis zur Schweizer Grenze. Aus dem anfänglichen Bewegungskrieg musste zum Stellungskrieg übergegangen werden. Die Armeen gruben sich ein, die Artillerie und die Maschinenwaffen wurden zum entscheidenden Faktor in der Kriegsführung. Die Materialschlacht war geboren! Keiner Partei gelang es, einen schlachtentscheidenden Durchbruch zu erzielen, um danach im Bewegungskrieg den Sieg erringen zu können. Im Gegenteil: Immer tiefer grub sich die Infanterie in die Erde, die Stellungen wurden festungsartig ausgebaut, verdrahtet, vermint und verbarrikadiert. Auch die äusserst verlustreichen Schlachten in Flandern, um Verdun und an der Somme brachten keiner Partei irgendwelche operativen Vorteile, geschweige denn eine Entscheidung. Sie brachten aber der Obersten Heeresleitung die Erkenntnis, dass der Krieg weder durch Materialschlachten noch durch Abnutzung oder Verblutung zu

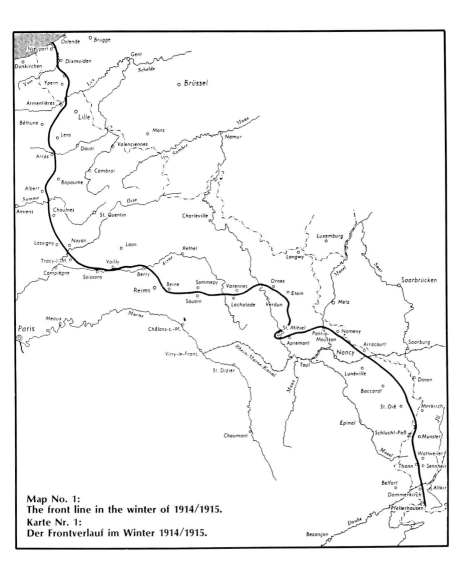

Map No. 1:
The front line in the winter of 1914/1915.
Karte Nr. 1:
Der Frontverlauf im Winter 1914/1915.

In 1916, the German 5th Army created Assault Battalion No. 3 under the command of Captain Rohr. Basically a training battalion, it stressed new assault tactics which concentrated heavy firepower in a very narrow front enabling highly mobile and well-armed troops to break through enemy weak spots and enable standard infantry units to exploit their breach.

gewinnen sei. Neue Taktiken, neuartige Waffen und eine neue Spezialtruppe mussten gefunden werden, um einen Durchbruch durch die starre Front erzielen zu können. So entstand 1916 bei der 5. Armee unter Führung von Hptm. Rohr das Sturmbataillon Nr. 3, ein Lehr-Bataillon. Hier wurde die Taktik der kleinen "Sturmkeile," des "Kampfes der verbundenen Waffen" und der exakten Abstimmung zwischen "Feuer und Bewegung" erprobt und geübt. Das

This theory was certainly not new, having been postulated by Frederick the Great who held that an inferior force could, if concentrated, exceed the strength of an enemy at a given point.

These assault troops were armed with mortars, flamethrowers, submachine guns and sacks of grenades and were taught to use these weapons at very close ranges. These training excercises, carried out before senior officers under simulated combat conditions using live ammunition, impressed the higher commands and in late July 1916, an assault detachment was duly ordered for the 2nd Army, its personnel to be trained by Assault Battalion Rohr until combat readiness was achieved.

The commanding officer of this new unit was Captain Hans Friedrichs who had acquired an excellent combat reputation on the Eastern Front by capturing the Russian fortress of Brest-Litovsk in Poland in August 1915 and the Serbian fortress of Belgrade in October of the same year.

In 1916, his assault detachment was organized as follows:
Detachment Staff
3 assault companies
1 machine gun company (6 MGs)
1 trench mortar detachment (6 light TMs)
1 close support gun battery (6 guns)
1 flamethrower platoon (6 small FTs)

In early September, after many difficulties in obtaining the required equipment and supplies, specialized training was begun at Etaves, approximately

---

Bataillon wurde hierbei nicht als geschlossener Verband, sondern in Stosstrupps eingesetzt, die, ausgerüstet mit Maschinengewehren, Granat- und Flammenwerfern, in exakter Abstimmung mit den schweren Waffen auf die Sturmsekunde genau in die vorderste Stellung einbrachen, sie aufrollten und so die Voraussetzungen zum weiteren Durchbruch schufen. Der Erfolg der Stosstrupps lag also in der schnellen Überwindung des feindlichen Sperrfeuers durch exakte Feuerunterstützung, in der Überraschung sowie in der exakten Zusammenarbeit zwischen den Sturmtrupps und der sie unterstützenden Infanteriegeschütze. Besonderer Wert wurde in der Ausbildung deshalb auf die hohe Treffsicherheit der auf kurze Entfernung schiessenden Infanteriegeschütze, Minen- und Granatwerfer gelegt. Diese Taktik des Angriffs mit begrenztem Ziel wurde von der Lehrtruppe immer und immer wieder nach genauester Erkundung, Einweisung und Befehlsgebung im scharfen Schuss an der Westfront erprobt und der höchsten militärischen Führung vorgeführt.

Ende Juli 1916 befahl das AOK 2 für die 2. Armee die Aufstellung einer Sturmabteilung. Es wurden zunächst die Offiziere, Unteroffiziere und Richtschützen der neu aufzustellenden Abteilung zum Sturmbataillon Rohr kommandiert und dort für ihre neue Verwendung vorbereitet. Hauptmann Hans Friedrichs wurde als neuer Kommandeur der Sturmabteilung der 2. Armee ausgewählt. Er hatte sich bereits bei der Einnahme der Festungen Brest-Litowsk (August 1915) und Belgrad (Oktober 1915) einen Namen gemacht. Damals drang er als Bataillonsführer des Res. Inf. Rgts. Nr. 203 mit seinem

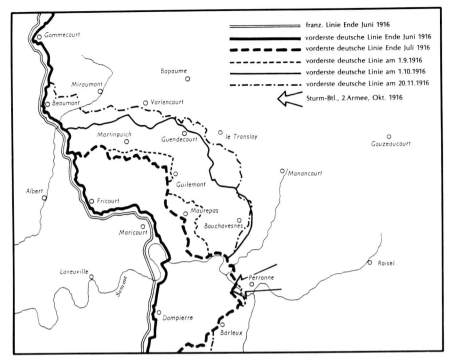

Map No. 2: The Somme battle - 1916.
Karte Nr. 2: Die Somme-Schlacht - 1916.

15km north of St. Quentin. By late September, the detachment consisted of 31 officers, 896 NCOs and men and 125 horses.

The tactical situation of the 11th Reserve Division in late October 1916 necessitated the first operation of the detachment. The controlling heights at Maisonette, south of Peronne, permitted the enemy to observe and effectively bombard the German lines. The capture of these heights was urgently requested. Supported by portions of the division (Infantry Regiment 395, two companies of Infantry Regiment 156 and two companies of Infantry Regiment 10), the 2nd Army's Assault Detachment attacked the heights, supported very effectively by concentrated artillery fire and a feint attack by Infantry Regi-

---

Bataillon als erster in die Festung ein und hisste auf der Zitadelle die deutsche Fahne. Seine Sturmabteilung wurde im August 1916 wie folgt gegliedert:

Abt-Stab

3 Sturm-Kompanien

1 MG-Kompanie (6 MG's)

1 Minenwerfer-Abteilung (6 le MW)

1 Infanteriegeschütz-Batterie (6 Geschütze)

1 Flammenwerfer-Zug (6 kleine FW)

Nach vielen organisatorischen Schwierigkeiten der Material- und Personalbeschaffung, der Unterbringung und Einrichtung von Ausbildungs- und

17

ment 156. Within 30 minutes, the heights were taken. Out of nine officers and 229 men engaged, total losses amounted to one dead, four missing and 28 wounded. In its baptism of fire, the new unit and its tactics had proven to be a great success.

In late November 1916, the detachment was disbanded, its elements serving as cadre for Assault Battalion No. 6 (6th Army) and Assault Battalion No. 7 (7th Army) and after December 4, 1916, these were organized as follows:

Battalion Staff (Garrison Bosmont)
2 assault companies
1 machine gun company
1 trench mortar company
1 close support gun battery
1 flamethrower platoon
Strength: 24 officers, 848 NCOs and men and 167 horses.

During the ensuing battles around Chemin des Dames in 1917 and the decisive battles at Souissons, Reims and Aisne in 1918, the battalion proved successful and became the model for other assault battalions and infantry regiments. Tactics were constantly being improved with the addition of aerial reconnaissance, increased artillery support and the use of surprise. Major Friedrichs could honestly say to his troops, "The assault battalion on the ground is as good as the fighter pilot in the sky!"

Übungsplätzen, konnte Anfang September in Etaves (ca. 15km nördlich St. Quentin) mit der Ausbildung begonnen werden. Ende September war die Abteilung mit 31 Offizieren, 896 Unteroffizieren und Mannschaften und 125 Pferden aufgestellt.

Die taktische Lage bei der 11. Res. Division erforderte Ende Oktober 1916 den ersten Einsatz: Angriff mit begrenztem Ziel. Zurück zuerobern waren die beherrschenden Maisonette-Höhen südl. Peronne, von denen der Gegner die deutschen Stellungen einsehen und wirkungsvoll beschiessen konnte. Um aber günstige Abwehrstellungen zu besitzen, musste die 11. Res. Division die Maisonette-Höhen erobern. Unterstützt durch Teile der Division (I.R. 359, 2 Kp. I.R. 156, 2 Kp. I.R. 10) trat die Sturmabteilung der 2. Armee mit 9 Stosstrupps am 29.10.1916 an. Der Angriff wurde sowohl artilleristisch als auch durch einen geschickt angelegten Scheinangriff vom I.R. 156 wirkungsvoll unterstützt. Schon nach knapp 30 Minuten wurde die befohlene Linie genommen! Die neue Taktik und Technik der Stosstrupps hatte sich voll bewährt! Bei einem Einsatz von 9 Offizieren, 229 Soldaten hatte die Abteilung nur 1 Toten, 4 Vermisste und 28 Verwundete zu beklagen.

Ende November 1916 wurde die Abteilung aufgelöst und diente als Stamm für das Sturmbataillon Nr. 6 (6. Armee) und das Sturmbataillon Nr. 7 (7. Armee), das nun ab 04.12.1916 wie folgt gegliedert war:

Btl-Stab (Standort Bosmont)
2 Sturm-Kp

1 MG-Kp

It should be noted that the battalion also had its failures, usually caused by incorrect timing of the battalion's commitment as well as the ensuing loss of surprise. The rolling artillery barrages were not always on target and when local successes were achieved, they were not always supported by stronger elements.

Major Friedrichs, commander of Assault Battalion No. 7.
Major Friedrichs, Kommandeur Sturmbataillon Nr. 7.

1 Minenwerfer-Kp
1 Infanterie-Geschütz-Bttr Nr. 4
1 Flammenwerfer-Zug
Stärke: 24 Offiziere, 848 Unteroffiziere und Mannschaften, 167 Pferde.

Bei den weiteren Kämpfen des Bataillons, vor allem bei den Kämpfen um den Chemin des Dames 1917 und den Entscheidungsschlachten in Frankreich bei Souissons, Reims, Aisne 1918, hat sich das Bataillon immer wieder bewährt und wurde Vorbild für andere Sturmbataillone und Infanterieregimenter. Die Taktik wurde verfeinert, die Luftaufklärung vermehrt genutzt, der artilleristische Anteil des Bataillons erweitert und die Überraschung stets eingeplant. Aber auch Misserfolge sind in der Bataillonschronik zu verzeichnen, und zwar immer dann, wenn diese Spezialtruppe nicht richtig eingesetzt wurde oder die Überraschung verschenkt, die Feuerwalze nicht richtig abgestimmt war oder örtliche, bitter erkämpfte Erfolge nicht genutzt wurden. Die Erfolge des Sturmbataillons waren neben der neuen Taktik vor allem auf die realistische, harte Ausbildung im scharfen Schuss auf dem Sturm-Übungsplatz Bosmont zurückzuführen. Hier hatte das Bataillon immer wieder in Lehrvorführungen vor hohen und höchsten Truppenführern und Regierungsabordnungen die Wirkung der Stosstrupptechnik zu demonstrieren. Der hohe Ausbildungs- und Einsatzstand Ende 1917 war nicht zuletzt auf die günstige Personalauswahl zurückzuführen. Ungeeignete Führer und Soldaten wurden sehr schnell wieder zurückversetzt. So konnte Major Friedrichs zu Recht zu seinem Bataillon sagen: "Was die

19

Training with live ammunition at Bosmont.
Stosstruppausbildung im scharfen Schuss in Bosmont.

Training behind the front near Sedan, May 1917.

Übung hinter der Front, bei Sedan, Mai 1917.

Getting their orders, 1916.
Befehlsempfang, 1916.

Trench mortar squad.
Granatwerfertrupp.

Unteroffizier Thiel and his mortar squad.
Unteroffizier Thiel mit seiner Granatwerferbedienung.

Medium trench mortar.
Mittlerer Minenwerfer.

75mm trench mortar, Western Front.
75mm Grabenmörser, Westfront.

Heavy flamethrower.
Grosser Flammenwerfer.

Light flamethrower in action.
Kleiner Flammenwerfer im Einsatz.

An infantry assault gun.
Infanterie-Begleitgeschütz.

The battalion's umpires for fire support by
infantry assault guns.
Bataillonsschiedsrichter für das
Wettkampfschiessen der Infanterie
Begleitgeschütze.

An infantry assault gun being moved into position.
Infanteriegeschütz geht in Stellung.

In mid-1917, the strength of Assault Battalion No. 7 was enlarged to approximately 1,500 soldiers and 500 horses and was organized as follows:

3 assault companies
2 machine gun companies
1 flamethrower company
1 flamethrower platoon
4 close support gun batteries

The attacks of the battalion in 1917 in the Chemin des Dames area were carried out successfully by following the now-proven formula:

accurate reconnaissance
concealed jumping-off positions
intense and precisely timed artillery barrages on the target
surprise assault carried out quickly, and
violent destruction of any resistance.

One drawback of this tactic was that it proved to be inflexible in the event of the unexpected, such as the introduction of tanks on a large scale at the battle of Cambrai on November 20, 1917. To counter this new weapon, the battalion developed two mobile batteries which consisted of support guns carried on trucks for rapid deployment. In critical situations, these guns were actually fired while still on the trucks.

In 1918, Assault Battalion No. 7, under the command of Major Friedrichs, was employed in the area of the 2nd Army during the major "Michael" offen-

---

Jagdflieger am Himmel, das seid ihr, die Stosstrupps auf der Erde." Mitte 1917 war das Sturmbataillon Nr. 7 auf rund 1500 Soldaten und 500 Pferde angewachsen und gliederte sich in:

3 Sturm-Kompanien
2 MG-Kompanien
1 Flammenwerfer-Kompanie
1 Flammenwerferzug
4 Infanterie-Geschütz-Batterien.

Die weiteren Kämpfe des Sturmbataillons Nr. 7 im Jahr 1917 im Bereich des Chemin des Dames, Angriff mit begrenztem Ziel, gewaltsame Aufklärung, verliefen immer wieder nach gleichem Schema: Versteckte, unbemerkte Bereitstellung - schlagartiges, ganz kurzes Artilleriefeuer zum Niederhalten des Feindes, besonders an den Einbruchstellen - überraschender Einbruch in die feindliche Abwehrzone im schnellsten Lauf - brutales Überrennen und Niederkämpfen jeglichen Widerstandes durch die Sturmkeile, dabei engstes Zusammenwirken und Unterstützen des Angriffs durch zahlreiche, dem Angriffsweg folgende Infanteriegeschütze - genau auf die Sekunde gestellte Uhren - schnellste, lückenlose Abwehrbereitschaft nach erfolgtem Sturm mit möglichst zahlreichen Maschinenwaffen ganz vorne! Dieses Verfahren war jedoch bei unvorhergesehenen Ereignissen wenig flexibel. Eine Führung und Veränderung des Angriffsplanes war ab Angriffsbeginn nicht mehr durchführbar. Hierzu fehlte noch das Führungsmittel Funk. Andererseits reagierte das Sturmbataillon Nr. 7 auf die neue Bedrohung durch Tanks, die

During the march to the front.
Auf dem Vormarsch.

Loading infantry guns onto trucks.
Infanteriegeschütze beim Verladen.

Motorized infantry guns on their way to the front.
Infanteriegeschütze auf der Fahrt zur Front.

Captured British Mk 4 tank used for training purposes.
Erbeuteter Tank für Übungszwecke.

sive. The successes of the battalion during the attack at Amigny and Sinceny on April 6 of that year resulted in the awarding of the Knight's Cross of the Hohenzollern House Order with Swords to First Lieutenant Foertsch, commander of the 1st Assault Company. To date, this award had only been given to the battalion commander.

In May of 1918, the battalion was divided into eight "assault blocks" and employed by several divisions of Army High Command 7 (AOK 7). As was an-

erstmalig im grösseren Umfang am 20.11.1917 bei der Tankschlacht bei Cambrai eingesetzt wurden. Dem Bataillon wurden zur Panzerabwehr zwei Kraftwagen-Batterien zugeteilt. Die Infanteriegeschütze wurden auf den Lastkraftwagen transportiert und konnten notfalls auch von diesen schiessen. 1918 wurde das Sturmbataillon Nr. 7 unter Führung von Major Friedrichs im Rahmen der 2. Armee bei der Grossoffensive "Michael" eingesetzt. Die Kampferfolge des Bataillons, besonders die Erfolge im Angriff auf Amigny

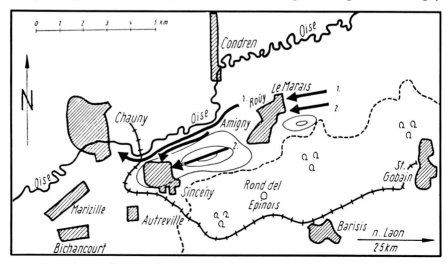

Map No. 3: The attack on April 6, 1918.
Karte Nr. 3: Angriff am 06.04.1918.

Kaiser Wilhelm II.

The Kaiser visits the assault battalion.
Abschreiten der Front.

ticipated, these assault blocks suffered heavy losses but were so successful that Lieutenants Fangauf, Feninger and Neumann were awarded the Knight's Cross of the Hohenzollern House Order with Swords.

On June 17, 1918, HM the Kaiser inspected the thinned ranks of the battalion and proudly said, "I have always heard good things about Assault Battalion No. 7. Everywhere it faced the enemy, it did its duty. I hope you will continue to be the same as you have been until now...a fright to the enemy." The next day, the battalion was transferred to its new quarters in Bourg et

und Sinceny am 06.04.1918, wurden durch die Verleihung des "Ritterkreuzes des Königlichen Hausordens von Hohenzollern mit Schwertern" an Oberleutnant Foertsch, Führer der 1. Sturmkompanie, gewürdigt. Diese Auszeichnung trug bislang im Bataillon nur der Bataillonskommandeur.

Wie bei allen Elitetruppen liess sich im Mai 1918 nicht vermeiden, dass das Bataillon nicht geschlossen, sondern ab 16.05.1918 in 8 "Sturmblocks" eingeteilt und bei verschiedenen Divisionen des AOK 7 eingesetzt wurde. Wie erwartet errangen diese Sturmblocks solche Erfolge, dass Lt. Fangauf, Feninger und Neumann ebenfalls mit dem "Ritterkreuz des königl. Hausordens von Hohenzollern mit Schwertern" ausgezeichnet wurden. Auch der

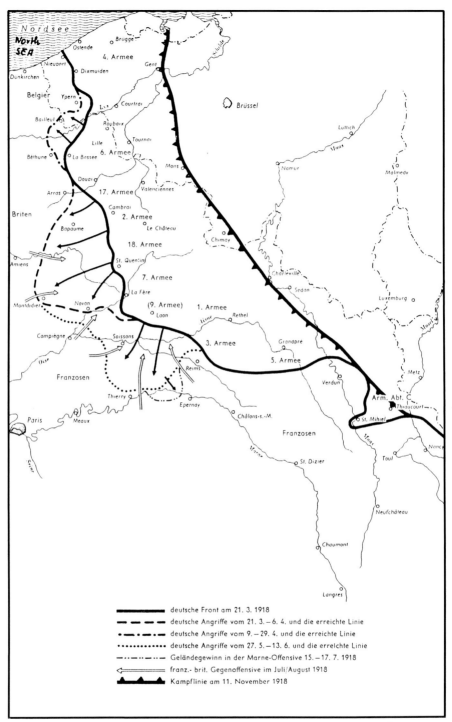

Map No. 4: The last German offensive in 1918 and the counter-attacks until November 11, 1918.
Karte Nr. 4: Die letzte deutsche Offensive im Westen im Frühjahr 1918 und die alliierte Gegenoffensive bis zum Waffenstillstand am 11. November 1918.

Comin (near Aisne) where it began accelerated training for the pending offensive actions on the Marne and in the Champagne.

Once again, the battalion was divided up, this time into five "assault blocks," and was given the difficult mission of attacking across the Marne River. The enemy had expected the German offensive and had heavily fortified their primary and secondary defensive positions, causing high losses to the attacking units. This proved to be the last German offensive in the West.

Bundesarchiv

An assault block before the attack.
Stosstrupp vor dem Sturm.

Kaiser und Oberste Kriegsherr besuchte und besichtigte das stark dezimierte Bataillon und würdigte dessen Leistungen und Opfer beim Abschied am 17.06.1918 mit den Worten: "...Ich habe vom Sturmbataillon 7 immer nur Gutes gehört. Überall, wo das Bataillon dem Feinde entgegengetreten ist, da hat es jedesmal seine Schuldigkeit getan. Ich hoffe, dass Ihr das bleiben werdet, was Ihr bis jetzt gewesen seid: ein Schrecken der Feinde." Tags darauf verlegte das komplette Sturmbataillon Nr. 7 in sein neues Quartier in Bourg et Comin (bei Aisne) und mit der Ausbildung konnte, wenn auch nicht so günstig wie in Bosmont, wieder begonnen werden, denn die Angriffsschlachten an der Marne und in der Champagne standen bevor.

Wieder wurde das Sturmbataillon Nr. 7 in 5 Sturmblocks aufgeteilt, wobei der Auftrag schwierig war: Angriff über Gewässer. Obgleich der Gegner die deutsche Offensive erwartet hatte und entsprechende Verteidigungsmassnahmen sowohl in den vordersten Stellungen als auch in der Tiefe vorgenommen hatte, gelang ein Einbruch bis zu den zweiten, weit hinten angelegten Stellungen, allerdings unter hohen Verlusten für die Sturmblocks. Die Angriffsschlachten an der Marne und in der Champagne waren die letzten deutschen Angriffsoperationen im Westen (Karte 4). Danach

The Allies then counterattacked, supported by superior numbers of tanks and aircraft. These battles of attrition depleted the strength of Assault Battalion No. 7 which was then reenforced by elements of the disbanded Assault Battalion No. 12. The morale and fighting spirit of the battalion remained unbroken even as the German army became more demoralized.

It was employed again and again by the High Command, providing security against saboteurs and deserters in the rear area as well as utilization in defensive positions in front of the 7th Army. The appearance of a heavily-armed, elite unit with perfect discipline went far in stabilizing the area under the battalion's control.

But by this time, all was lost and its last duty before the armistice on November 11, 1918, was as a regimental-strength army reserve, delaying detachment.

---

kam die Gegenoffensive der Alliierten, reichlich durch amerikanische Tanks und Flugzeuge unterstützt. Nach den verlustreichen Schlachten wurde das Sturmbataillon Nr. 7 durch das Sturmbataillon Nr. 12 ergänzt. Die Moral und die Kampfkraft war trotz der zahlreichen Auflösungserscheinungen im Feldheer ungebrochen, so dass das Bataillon immer wieder für Sonderaufgaben durch die Oberste Heeresleitung eingesetzt werden musste: Sicherungsaufgaben im Hinterland, Verteidigung an der Front bei der 7. Armee und Ordnungsaufgaben gegen zurückströmende Deserteure und Saboteure. Zum Glück reichte hier schon allein das Auftauchen eines schwerbewaffneten, hochdisziplinierten Eliteverbandes. Der letzte Einsatzbefehl vor dem Waffenstillstand am 11.11.1918 sah den Einsatz des auf Regimentsstärke gebrachten "Detachement Friedrichs" als Armeereserve bzw. "Nachkommando" vor.

Map No. 5: Locations and battles.
Karte Nr. 5: Standorte und Einsätze.

---

② Locations and missions of Assault Battalion, 2nd Army.

⑦ Locations and missions of Assault Battalion No. 7.

② Standorte und Einsatzräume Sturmbataillon 2. Armee.

⑦ Standorte und Einsatzräume Sturmbataillon 7.

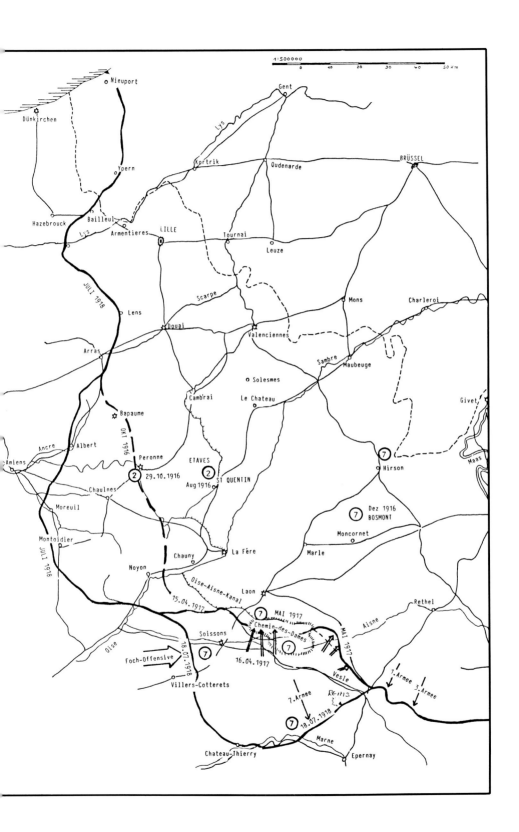

The Postwar Period

Nachkriegszeit

After the armistice came into effect, the detachment marched in perfect order and under arms from Remagen to Marburg where it had to restore public order and provide security against radical political groups. It was then sent to Kassel to provide security for the German High Command. In February 1919, the battleworthy and famous Assault Battalion No. 7 was deactivated. Its remnants, along with parts of Assault Battalion No. 5, built up two infantry companies with the mission of guard detachment for the German High Command (Wachkommando OHL), and later transferred to Coburg/Pomerania. From this detachment, "Freikorps Field Marshal v. Hindenburg" was formed and assigned to the supreme headquarters under the leadership of Captain i.G. Otto. Initially, it was approximately battalion strength, but was later expanded to regimental size. The original battalion retained the title of "Assault Battalion" whereas the 2nd Company was entitled "2nd Assault Company" under the command of First Lieutenant Foertsch. The company wore the number "7" on its shoulder straps. Major Friedrichs was transferred to the Reichswehr and was active in different commands until 1929 (II/I.R.115, I.R.5, III./I.R.8 and commander of the training area at Ohrdruf). He retired from the Reichswehr as a Generalmajor on March 31, 1929, and became the

Mit Inkrafttreten des Waffenstillstandes marschierte das Detachement in voller Ordnung und unter Waffen über Remagen nach Marburg, wo schnell die öffentliche Ordnung und Sicherheit gegen radikale politische Gruppen wiederhergestellt werden konnte. Danach erfolgte ein weiterer Einsatz als Schutztruppe des Grossen Hauptquartieres in Kassel. Februar 1919 wurde das bewährte und durch seine Leistungen berühmte Sturmbataillon Nr. 7 demobilisiert. Aus den Resten sowie Teilen des Sturmbataillons Nr. 5 wurde das "Wachkommando OHL" mit 2 Infanteriekompanien aufgestellt und nach Kolberg/Pommern verlegt.

Dort entstand aus dem "Wachkommando" das der OHL unmittelbar unterstehende "Freikorps Feldmarschall v. Hindenburg" unter Führung des damaligen Hauptmann i.G. Otto. Zuerst hatte es etwa Bataillonsstärke. Später wurde es zu Regimentsstärke ausgebaut, wobei das zuerst aufgestellte Bataillon die Bezeichnung "Sturmbataillon" behielt. Die 2. Kompanie wurde mit der Bezeichnung "2. Sturmkompanie" unter der Führung des Oberleutnant Foertsch gebildet. Die Kompanie trug auf den Achselklappen die Nummer 7. Major Friedrichs selbst wurde in die Reichswehr übernommen und war bis 1929 in verschiedenen Kommandos (II/I.R. 115, I.R. 5, III/I.R. 8, Kdt. Truppenübungsplatz Ohrdruf) tätig. Nachdem er als Generalmajor am 31.03.1929 die Reichswehr verlassen hatte, war er von 1934 bis 1945 Oberbürgermeister der alten Soldatenstadt Potsdam. Während dieser Zeit entstand

Collar insignia of the
Freikorps von Hindenburg.
Kragenabzeichen des
Freikorps von Hindenburg.

Storm troops of Freikorps Field Marshall
von Hindenburg. Von Hindenburg is at left
and Lt. Ristow is at right, front row,
standing.
Sturmgrenadiere im Freikorps
Feldmarschall von Hindenburg. Links: von
Hindenburg, rechts: Lt. Ristow.

Lord Mayor of Potsdam. During this period he developed a deep friendship
with Major Richard Heidrich, who was tactics instructor at the Potsdam Officers' Academy.

It is understandable, therefore, that Major Heidrich would have been exposed to and have accepted the traditions of the elite Assault Battalion No. 7
when he subsequently became the battalion commander of the new army airborne unit.

---

die enge Freundschaft zu Major Heidrich, der als Taktiklehrer an der
Kreigsschule Potsdam tätig war. Dadurch ist verständlich, dass Major
Heidrich als Kompaniechef bzw. Bataillonskommandeur der Fallschirminfan-
terie die Tradition des elitären Sturmbataillons Nr. 7 übernahm. Somit hatte
auch die junge Waffengattung der Fallschirminfanterie an die Tradition des
Kaiserheeres angeknüpft.

General Friedrichs. After his service in the Reichswehr, he became the Lord Mayor of Potsdam. There, he became close friends with Major Heidrich, the first commander of the Army Airborne Infantry Battalion.

General Friedrichs. Nach seiner Pensionierung wurde er Bürgermeister von Potsdam und Freund von Major Heidrich, dem ersten Kommandeur des Fallschirminfanteriebataillons.

Major Richard Heidrich.

THE HONOR LIST
of the Sturmbattalions of World War I

Unit	Date established[1]	Authorized by
Sturmbtl. No. 1	Dec. 4, 1916	Army Command 1
⋮	⋮	⋮
Sturmbtl. No. 5[2]	⋮	⋮
⋮	⋮	⋮
⋮	⋮	⋮

[1] Besides these assault battalions, there were more "Sturmabteilungen" (Assault Battalions) belonging to divisions. They had the same numbers as their divisions but are not listed in this honor list because they were not independent units.

[2] Initially built-up on February 28, 1915 as Sturmabt. Gaede, it was then changed to Sturmbataillon Calsow, then to Sturmbataillon Rohr.

EHRENTAFEL

der Sturmbataillone des ersten Weltkrieges

Formation	aufgestellt [1) am	durch
Sturmbataillon Nr. 1	4. 12. 1916	Armee-Oberkommando 1
Sturmbataillon Nr. 2	2. 11. 1916	Armee-Oberkommando 3
Sturmbataillon Nr. 3	8. 7. 1916	—
Sturmbataillon Nr. 4	9. 12. 1916	Armee-Oberkommando 4
Sturmbataillon Nr. 5 [2)	11. 3. 1916	Armee-Abteilung Gaede
Sturmbataillon Nr. 6	4. 12. 1916	Armee-Oberkommando 6
Sturmbataillon Nr. 7	4. 12. 1916	Armee-Oberkommando 7
Sturmbataillon Nr. 8	28. 12. 1916	Armee-Oberkommando Südarmee
Sturmbataillon Nr. 9	18. 12. 1916	Armee-Oberkommando 9
Sturmbataillon Nr. 10	28. 12. 1916	Oberkommando Heeresgruppe Eichhorn
Sturmbataillon Nr. 11	18. 12. 1916	Oberkommando Heeres-Gruppe Linsingen
Sturmbataillon Nr. 12	28. 12. 1916	Oberkommando Heeresgruppe Woyrsch
Sturm-Kompanie Nr. 13	28. 12. 1916	General-Kommando I. Armeekorps
Sturmbataillon Nr. 14	1. 1. 1917	Armee-Abteilung v. Strantz
Sturmbataillon Nr. 15	23. 12. 1916	Armee-Abteilung A
Sturmbataillon Nr. 16	23. 12. 1916	Armee-Abteilung B
Sturmbataillon Nr. 17	19. 1. 1917	—
Sturmbataillon Nr. 18	7. 8. 1917	Oberkommando Heeresgruppe Eichhorn
Sturmbataillon Heeresgruppe Herzog Albrecht	1. 10. 1917	Oberkommando Heeresgruppe Herzog Albrecht

[1] Außer den vorstehenden Sturmtruppen befanden sich bei mehreren Divisionen Sturmabteilungen (Stoßtrupps), die nach der betreffenden Divisionsnummer benannt waren. Sie sind hier nicht aufgeführt, da es sich um keine etatsmäßigen Formationen handelte.

[2] Bereits am 28. Februar 1915 aufgestellt als Sturmabteilung Gaede, dann umbenannt in Sturmbataillon Calsow, dann in Sturmbataillon Rohr.

THE ARMY AIRBORNE INFANTRY COMPANY

DIE FALLSCHIRMINFANTERIEKOMPANIE

Airborne Development Abroad

Entwicklung der Fallschirmtruppe im Ausland

Universal conscription was reintroduced on March 16, 1935, and the new Wehrmacht was quickly expanded. In November of that year, the Luftwaffe was established and this new service utilized the experiences and knowledge gained by the clandestine German air units during their cooperation with the Russian military forces. In 1926, Captain Minov of the Red Army observed the use of the Irvin parachute as sporting equipment in the U.S. He grasped the potential for military use and took it back to the Soviet Union. On August 2, 1930, the official inauguration date of the Russian airborne forces, a group of twelve parachutists jumped as a unit and in September, a similar feat was performed by ten soldiers under the command of Lieutenant Moshkowsky. This tactical move was to eliminate an army command post, and proved so successful that the development of this form of warfare received immediate attention from higher authority. In 1931, the future Marshal Tuchachevsky, as public vice-commissar for army matters, developed the idea of "deep com-

Mit Wiedereinführung der allgemeinen Wehrpflicht am 16.03.1935 und der damit verbundenen raschen Vergrösserung der Wehrmacht und Aufstellung der Luftwaffe befahl im November 1935 das Oberkommando der Luftwaffe die Schaffung einer Fallschirmtruppe. Somit nutzte sie die Erfahrungen und Erkenntnisse, die die geheime deutsche Luftwaffe in ihrer Zusammenarbeit mit den russischen Streitkräften gemacht hatte.

Schon 1926 beobachtete der Hauptmann der Roten Armee Minov in den USA den Einsatz des Irvin-Fallschirmes als Sportgerät. Die Idee, Fallschirme für militärische Zwecke zu nutzen, wurde von ihm in Russland aufgegriffen und konsequent weiterbetrieben. So sprang am 02.08.1930, dem "Geburtstag" der russ. Fallschirmtruppe, eine Gruppe von 12 Fallschirmschützen geschlossen ab, im September eine weitere Gruppe von 10 Soldaten unter Führung des Leutnant Moshkowsky. Seine taktische Manöveraufgabe, ein Armeekommando auszuschalten, löste er so erfolgreich, dass die taktisch-

bat" or behind-the-lines strikes. This form of combat jump was of great importance as it negated the defensive strength of the front line. It should be noted that in tandem with airborne development, the Soviets were also achieving success with a military air transport concept. Red Army soldiers were airlifted into hostile territory for reconnaissance purposes against the White Basmatschen tribes which threatened the Soviet Union from Afghanistan, and were later recovered after their mission. Also, in 1929, the town of Garm, controlled by the Basmatschen, was taken by Soviet troops after being reinforced by air with 45 soldiers armed with machine guns.

The opportunities evident in aircraft and parachutes as a military operation factor caused the Soviets to transform their 11th Infantry Division into an experimental airborne unit in 1931. In the following year, "Airborne Troops" officially became a new branch of service and in 1933, a parachute instructor school was established in Tushino. At the same period, parachuting as a sport also became extremely popular in Russia with more than 1,000 jump towers being erected in parks and leisure facilities.

The military development of the parachute also progressed rapidly with 900 parachutists employed in maneuvers in 1934 and 1,200 parachutists and 5,700 air landing infantry utilized in 1936. The latter was a major maneuver near Kiev and the new "vertical, strategic enclosure" concept was viewed by numerous international guests and attachés.

---

technische Entwicklung rasante Fortschritte machte, zumal 1931 der spätere Marschall Tuchatschewski als stellvertretender Volkskommissar für Angelegenheiten der Armee die Idee des "tiefen Gefechts" entwickelte. Bei diesem Prinzip, die Verteidigung eines Gegners gleichzeitig in ihrer gesamten Tiefe zu bekämpfen, kam dem Gedanken der Luftlandung grosse Bedeutung zu. Schon 1928, parallel zur Entwicklung einer eigenständigen Fallschirmtruppe, hatte man praktische Erfolge im Militärischen Lufttransport gesammelt: Rotarmisten wurden zur Aufklärung gegen Weisse Batmatschenbanden, die von Afghanistan die Sowjetrepublik bedrohten, im Lufttransport eingeflogen und wieder aufgenommen. 1929 wurde die ebenfalls durch Basmatschenbanden belagerte Garnisonstadt Garm durch im Lufttransport herangebrachte 45 Rotarmisten mit Maschinengewehren verstärkt. Dieses plötzliche Auftauchen schwerbewaffneter Soldaten war in diesen regionalen Kämpfen letztlich die Entscheidung zugunsten der Sowjetregierung. Beide technischen Möglichkeiten, das Flugzeug und den Fallschirm zu militärischen Zwecken zu nutzen, führten 1931 zur Umwandlung der 11. Schützendivision in eine Versuchs-Luftlandeeinheit. 1932 wurde die "Luftlandetruppe" offiziell eine neue Waffengattung, die ab 1933 auch über eine Fallschirminstruktoren-Schule in Tushino verfügte. Gleichzeitig begann ein grosser Propagandafeldzug für das sportliche Fallschirmspringen - mit grossem Erfolg! Fallschirmsport war fast schon Volkssport. Über 1000 Sprungtürme entstanden in Parks und Freizeitanlagen!

Und auch die militärische Entwicklung ging zügig voran: 1934 wurden schon 900 Fallschirmjäger bei Manövern eingesetzt, 1936 sogar 1200 und 5700 Luft-

Parachutists jumped free-fall from 600-700 meters, and occupied an airport approximately 20km behind "enemy lines" and established the prerequisites for the landing of air-assault infantry by transport planes. On July 16, 1932, a Soviet soldier, Jeudokimow, jumped free-fall, without oxygen, from a height of 6,920 meters (115 seconds of free-fall), and on June 16, 1934, from 8,000 meters with oxygen. Without a doubt, the Soviet Union was the greatest airborne power at this time.

At the beginning of the German-Russo war in June of 1941, the Soviets had three airborne corps, each with three airborne infantry brigades and three air-assault infantry brigades being trained in airborne tactics and equipped with special weapons.

The development of the parachute in Russia from 1928 onwards was critically observed by the Germans. Initially, the German Army did not draw any significant conclusions from their observations of these Russian developments, but Italy, which had been experimenting with parachutes since 1927, did practice air transport and aerial resupply of ground forces by parachute. In the Ethiopian campaign of 1936, Italy dropped 72 live goats and two oxen to their ground combat forces because dressed meat decomposed very quickly in the desert heat.

---

landeinfanteristen. Dieses Grossmanöver im Raum Kiew vor internationalen Gästen und Attachés zeigte das neue Konzept der "vertikalen, strategischen Umfassung" der Roten Armee: Fallschirmjäger besetzten im Sprungeinsatz einen ca. 20km hinter den feindlichen Linien liegenden Flugplatz und schafften so die Voraussetzung für eine nachfolgende Luftlandung von Infanterie mit Transportflugzeugen. Die Fallschirmabsprünge erfolgten übrigens manuell aus 600-700 Metern. Und im manuellen Fallschirmspringen hatten die Russen beträchtliche Rekorde: Am 16.05.1932 sprang Jewdokimow manuell ohne Sauerstoff aus 6920 m Höhe (115 Sekunden freier Fall), am 16.07.1934 mit Sauerstoff aus 8000 Metern. Zweifellos war die Sowjetunion damals die grösste Luftlandemacht: Sie verfügte zu Kriegsbeginn im Juni 1941 über 3 Luftlandekorps zu je 3 Fallschirmjäger-Brigaden und 3 in der Luftlandetechnik geschulte und ausgerüstete Infanteriebrigaden!

Die Entwicklung der russ. Fallschirmtruppe wurde in Deutschland mit Interesse beobachtet, wenngleich der spätere Oberbefehlshaber und Schöpfer der deutschen Fallschirmtruppe, General Kurt Student, der ja des öfteren noch als Hauptmann zum Flugplatz Lipezk (bei Woronesh) gereist war, zu dem Zeitpunkt noch andere Aufgaben hatte. Das Heer der deutschen Wehrmacht zog aus den Entwicklungen in Russland und Italien zunächst keine Konsequenzen.

Die italienischen Streitkräfte experimentierten übrigens auch schon ab 1927 mit Fallschirmspringern, nutzten aber hauptsächlich den Fallschirm für die Versorgung aus der Luft. So wurden im Abessinien-Feldzug 1936 u.a. 72 lebende Ziegen und 2 Ochsen per Fallschirm abgeworfen, weil Schlachtfleisch bei einer Hitze von über 60 Grad zu schnell verdarb.

Parachutists of the Luftwaffe

Die Fallschirmjäger der Deutschen Luftwaffe

In Germany, the first military unit trained as parachutists and attached to the 1st Battalion of "Regiment General Göring" was under Luftwaffe control. Also, the first airborne school of the Wehrmacht was at the airfield at Stendal under the command of Captain Immans and Senior Police officer Diete, both skilled parachutists. Diete had received his jump training in Russia and had acted as a rigger, dispatcher and jumpmaster. The first public employment of parachutists occurred at the Wehrmacht maneuvers at Bückeburg near Hamelin, on October 4, 1936.

So gebührt in Deutschland der Luftwaffe der Ruhm, als erste Teilstreitkraft Fallschirmjäger ausgebildet und im I. Bataillon des "Regimentes General Göring" zusammengefasst zu haben. Auch die erste Fallschirmspringer-Schule der Wehrmacht auf dem Flughafen Stendal gehörte zur Luftwaffe und hatte ab 01.02.1936 in Hauptmann Immans und Polizeimeister Diete bereits erfahrene Fallschirmspringer. (Diete hatte übrigens seine Ausbildung in Russland bekommen und fungierte sowohl als Fallschirmpacker als auch als Absetzer.) Trotz Improvisation konnte diese Schule bald die ersten Fallschirmjäger, wie sie bei der Luftwaffe im "Regiment General Göring" offiziell genannt wurden, ausbilden und das new geschaffene "Fallschirmschützenabzeichen der Luftwaffe" den ausgebildeten Jägern im Dezember 1936 verleihen.

Der erste öffentliche Einsatz von Fallschirmjägern im Rahmen eines Wehrmachtmanövers fand am 04.10.1936 bei Bückeburg/Hameln statt.

Stendal, the first home of the airborne infantry.
Stendal, der erste Friedensstandort der Fallschirminfanterie.

Army Airborne Infantry
Fallschirm-Infanterie

The successful demonstation of the Luftwaffe parachute unit to senior Wehrmacht officers initiated the development of airborne infantry for the army. Volunteers were recruited principally from infantry regiments and after strict selection procedures and testing for "parachute fitness for service," were marched to the newly-established Stendal facility where they were stationed at the "Albrecht the Bear" barracks.

On April 1, 1937, the official founding date for the Airborne Infantry Company, the new unit was in formation before its commander, Captain Zahn. As part of the instructional troops, the members carried a Gothic "L" (Lehr") on their shoulder straps and were subordinated to the inspector of the infantry. The company consisted of:

Company Squad (administration)

signal squad

three infantry platoons

one heavy platoon with:

> (The company was the 15th Company of the "Infantry Instruction Regiment" (therefore "L" was worn)).

    one heavy machine gun group

    one heavy trench mortar group

    one engineer group

After completing jump training at Stendal, the men of the Airborne Infantry Company, as they were officially titled, received their Army Parachute

---

Vermutlich war diese gelungene Vorführung vor der Wehrmachtsführung der auslösende Moment, nun endlich im Heer selbst mit der Aufstellung einer Fallschirminfanterie zu beginnen. Jedenfalls wurde in allen Heeresverbänden, vornehmlich bei den Infanterieregimentern, für Freiwillige geworben. Nach strengen Auswahlverfahren und Überprüfung auf "Fallschirmtauglichkeit" (ähnlich den Kriterien "Fliegertauglichkeit") wurden die Freiwilligen des Heeres zur neu aufzustellenden Fallschirminfanterie-Kompanie (F.I.K.) nach Stendal in das Barackenlager der "Albrecht-der-Bär-Kaserne" in Marsch gesetzt. Am 01.04.1937 - dem Geburtstag der F.I.K. - stand diese neue Einheit vor ihrem Kompaniechef, Hauptmann Zahn. Als Lehrtruppe[*] mit dem "L" auf den Schulterklappen unterstand sie dem Inspekteur der Infanterie. Die Kompanie war gegliedert in:

Kompanietrupp

Nachr. Trp.

3 Inf. Züge

1 schw. Zug mit:

> [*] 15.Kompanie des Infanterie-Lehrregiments, daher "L".

    1 sMG Gruppe

    1 sGrW Gruppe

    1 Pionier-Gruppe.

Nach erfolgreicher Sprungausbildung in Stendal bekamen die Männer der Fallschirm-Infanterie ein eigenes Abzeichen, das "Fallschirmschützen-

The first airborne infantry company commander, Hauptmann Zahn.

Der erste Kompaniechef der Fallschirminfanterie, Hauptmann Zahn.

A NCO shoulder strap with "L". The Army Airborne Infantry Company was part of the Infantry Experimental and Training Regiment at Döberitz.

Schulterstück eines Feldwebels des Infanterie-Lehrregiments in Döberitz, zu dem die Fallschirminfanterie-Kompanie ab 01.04.1937 gehörte.

Karl Esche, one of the first airborne infantrymen (note "L" on shoulder strap) and Army Parachute Badge.

Karl Esche, Angehöriger der Fallschirminfanterie-Kompanie ab 01.04.1937. (Beachte das "L" auf den Schulterstücken und das Fallschirmschützenabzeichen des Heeres.)

41

Army Parachute Badge.
Fallschirmschützenabzeichen
des Heeres.

Badge. The first training of the company was carried out between May 4 and June 3 of 1937 at which time it was intended to expand the unit to battalion strength. The commander of the new battalion was to be Major Richard Heidrich mentioned previously. He was an instructor at the Potsdam Officers' Academy when he was offered the command of the Company. He later wrote about the offer: "One day in 1937, a comrade of mine who had been posted as Ia to the inspector of the infantry, spoke to me at the regulars' table in a local pub. He told me of plans to establish an army parachute battalion of which one company was already in existance and indicated that I was slated to be commander. When I heard the word "parachute," I was mildly shocked and could not imagine what it entailed. He urged me to go to Stendal in civilian clothes and then proceeded to inform me about the organization of the Luftwaffe jump school. The next day I asked for a leave and drove to Stendal where I was given a tour. I had no feeling at this time for this new unit and said to myself, 'No, why should I give up a fine position in the infantry

---

abzeichen des Heeres." Der erste Lehrgang für die F.I.K. wurde vom 04.05. - 03.06.1937 durchgeführt. Zu dieser Zeit war schon geplant, die Kompanie auf Bataillonsstärke zu erweitern. Und der 2. Kompaniechef, bzw. der 1. Bataillonskommandeur des Fallschirm-Infanterie-Bataillons wurde im Sommer 1937 ebenfalls festgelegt: Major Richard Heidrich. Er war zu dem Zeitpunkt Lehrer an der Kriegsschule Potsdam, als ihm das Angebot gemacht wurde, Kommandeur eines Fallschirminfanterie-Bataillons zu werden. Er schrieb darüber: "Eines Tages, im Jahre 1937, sprach mich einer meiner Kameraden, der inzwischen als Ia zur Inspektion der Infanterie versetzt worden war, am Stammtisch an. Man beabsichtigte, eine Fallschirmtruppe aufzustellen, hätte bereits eine Kompanie, ich sei doch..., ob ich nicht usw. usw...Als ich das Wort Fallschirm hörte, bekam ich zunächst einen gelinden Schreck und sagte, ich könne mir darunter gar nichts vorstellen, worauf er sehr eilig drängte und mich bat, am nächsten Tag doch in Zivil nach Stendal zu fahren und mich an der dortigen Fallschirmschule der Luftwaffe orientieren

April 1, 1937: Formation of the Army Airborne Infantry Company in Stendal, "Albrecht the Bear" barracks.
01.04.1937: Aufstellung Fsch.Inf.Kp. (FIK) in Stendal, Albrecht der Bär-Kaserne.

branch?' A short time later, I visited Stendal on the occasion of the annual officers' school study tour. By that time it appeared that the infant had grown up. We got into a Ju52 transport and watched a jump from the air. Again, a creepy feeling about jumping out of a plane came over me, especially considering that I was 42 years old."

zu lassen. Ich erbat Urlaub von der Kriegsschule und fuhr los. Es wurde mir alles gezeigt. Ich hatte aber das Gefühl, dass die Sache noch sehr in primitiven Anfängen stecke und sagte in meinem Inneren: "Nein, warum sollst Du Deine an sich gesicherte und schöne Laufbahn bei der Infanterie aufgeben?" Kurze Zeit später besichtigte ich anlässlich der jährlichen Bildungsreise der Kriegsschule bei schönem Wetter auch die Fallschirmschule Stendal. Die

Shortly before Major Heidrich took over command of the airborne company in the autumn of 1937, it had its first jump-related accidents on August 20 and September 20 during the course of the fall maneuvers in Mecklenburg. These occurred in the presence of the spectators, including Major Heidrich. He remembered those accidents vividly and wrote of his impressions: "In the autumn of 1937 I had been posted to the Airborne Infantry Company as a Major. The new command got off to a bad start when I was a spectator at the fall maneuvers and a parachutist's static line became tangled on the rear skid of a JU52. After numerous attempts to free him, the lines were cut and the man fell to his death. As for the majority of the men of the airborne company, they were a rough group of individuals and more or less ignored me. I was finally told point blank that I would have to take the jump course before I could gain their respect and attention. I rejected the idea and declared that I would first establish proper discipline within the company by Christmas and then, would attend jump school and take the course required by every parachutist. The men would have to accept matters until spring of the following year.

The reorganization went as planned and I then went to jump school as the oldest student and had to endure the entire course in its entirety. I did my jumps and insisted on receiving no special treatment whatsoever. I jumped in various positions within the "stick," learned to pack the parachute after use and whatever else was required. With soldier's luck, I made my prescribed six

---

Sache liess sich da schon manierlicher an. Als wir aber in einer Springer-maschine mitfuhren und den Absprung ansahen, da kam doch wieder das Gruseln vor der Geschichte, denn ich war immerhin schon 42 Jahre alt."

Doch noch bevor Major R. Heidrich die Kompanie im Herbst 1937 über-nahm, hatte die F.I.K. die ersten tödlichen Sprungunfälle am 20.08. und am 20.09.1937 während des Herbstmanövers in Mecklenburg vor Zuschauern, un-ter denen auch Major Heidrich weilte. An diesen Vorfall und an seine ersten Eindrücke von der Fallschirminfanterie-Kompanie erinnerte sich Major Heidrich wie folgt: "Im Herbst 1937 wurde ich zur Fallschirminfanteriekom-panie versetzt als Major. Die Sache nahm einen schlechten Start insofern als ich als erstes das grosse Manöver in Meckenburg als Zuschauer mitmachen musste, wobei bei dem Absprung der Kompanie ein Mann an der Maschine hängen blieb und auch nach längeren Rettungsversuchen abgeschnitten wur-den musste und somit den Tod fand. Im übrigen war die Kompanie, nachdem ich mir die Sache näher besah, ein ziemlich toller Landsknechthaufen. Ich selbst wurde auch gar nicht anerkannt und von den Leuten völlig neben-sächlich behandelt. Man sagte mir glatt, ich solle erst mal springen. Ich nahm aber die Sache gelassen hin und erklärte der Kompanie, dass ich vom Herbst bis Weihnachten erst einmal organisatorisch und disziplinell Ordnung schaffen wolle, nach Weihnachten würde ich dann auf die Sprungschule gehen und wie jeder Soldat meinen Kursus absolvieren, so dass wir uns dann im Frühjahr nichts mehr vorzuwerfen hätten. Die Dinge liefen so, wie ich sie mir vorgenommen hatte. Auf der Sprungschule war ich der alte Herr, musste aber alles mitmachen wie die jungen Soldaten, die dort ausgebildet wurden,

Gefr. Bunke, who was fatally injured during a training jump on August 20, 1937.
Gefr. Bunke, tödlich verunglückt beim Sprungdienst am 20.08.1937.

Gefr. Seelbach lost his life on September 20, 1937 while jumping. All attempts to rescue him from the skid of a Ju-52 were in vain.
Gefr. Seelbach verlor bei einem Manöversprung trotz verschiedenster Rettungsversuche am 20.09.1937 sein Leben.

Funeral with military honors.
Beisetzung mit militärischen Ehren.

jumps and was never injured, although there were many other jumping injuries as soldiers landed on the hard, frozen ground of the airfield."

On June 1, 1938, the army took steps to expand the airborne company to battalion strength. While still company strength and under the command of Major Heidrich, the army's parachute unit participated in a naval maneuver with a jump onto the island of Borkum on June 21 and 22.

Besides the Parachute Badge of the army, members of the Airborne Infantry Battalion now wore "FI" (Fallschirm-Infanterie) on their shoulder straps. Although the Airborne Infantry Company and, in the beginning, the Battalion, was subordinated to the Inspector of Infantry, it soon came under the influence of the Luftwaffe's 7th Flying Division which controlled the parachute training, the equipment, and air transport. The commander of this unit, General Kurt Student, had clear cut goals and ideas for the new German airborne branch, one of which was to create a unified command under the Luftwaffe.

---

machte wie sie meine Übungssprünge, verbat mir ausdrücklich jede Extrawurst. Sprang mal als Erster, bald in der Mitte, bald als Letzter, lernte gründlich das Fallschirmpacken und was sonst noch dazugehört. Bei den sechs vorgeschriebenen Pflichtsprüngen hatte ich Soldatenglück entwickelt und mich nie verletzt, obgleich auf dem hartgefrorenen Flugplatz, auf dem damals noch zwei sogenannte "Härtesprünge" ausgeführt wurden, reichlich Sprungverletzungen vorkamen."

Ab 01.06.1938 traf das Heer und die F.I.K. vorbereitende Massnahmen zur Vergrösserung zum Bataillon. Noch als Kompanie nahmen die Heeresfallschirmschützen unter Führung von Major Heidrich am 21. und 22.06.1938 am Flottenmanöver teil und sprangen dabei auf die Insel Borkum. Neben dem Heeresfallschirmschützenabzeichen trugen die Angehörigen des F.I.B. das "FJ" auf den Schulterklappen.

Wenngleich die F.I.K. und anfangs auch noch das F.I.B. unmittelbar dem Inspekteur der Infanterie unterstanden, hielt bald die Luftwaffe in Form der "7. Fliegerdivision" in Fragen Ausbildung, Einsatz und Lufttransport ihre Hand auf das Heeres-Bataillon. (Die "7. Fliegerdivision" war eine Tarnbezeichnung für die noch in Entwicklung stehende 1. Fallschirmjäger-Division der Luftwaffe. Diese Numerierung und Bezeichnung war unverfänglich, weil es ja im Sommer 1938 tatsächlich sechs Fliegerdivisionen gab). Und ihr neuer Kommandeur, General Kurt Student, hatte klare Ziele und Vorstellungen von der neuen deutschen Fallschirmtruppe, die natürlich unter einheitlichem Luftwaffenkommando stehen sollte.

Hans Mordhorst, airborne infantryman from the 1st Co. (note old style shoulder straps).

Hans Mordhorst, Fallschirminfanterist in der 1. Komp./Fallschirminf. Btl.

The old style, angular shoulder strap with white embroidered, Gothic "Fl" for enlisted soldiers.

Die alte, eckige Form eines Mannschaftsschulterstückes mit dem verschlungenen, gotischen "Fl", in weiss gestickt.

Jakob Stephani.

Gefr. Franz Glössner. Note new style shoulder strap and number "1" on shoulder button indicating he is a member of the 1st Company.

Gefr. Franz Glössner. Beachte die neuen Schulterstücke mit dem "Fl" und die "1" auf dem Knopf, d.h. er gehört zur 1. Kompanie des Fallschirminfanterie-Bataillons.

The new, round form of shoulder strap. Die neue, runde Form der Schulterstücke.

Johannes Wüstner, 2nd Company. Johannes Wüstner, 2.Kompanie.

Eric Queen

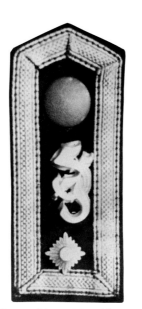

The "Fl" in metal for NCOs with Portepee (silver) and officers (gold).
Das "Fl" Abzeichen in Metall für Unteroffizier m.P. in silber und Offiziere in gold.

Eric Queen

Equipment

Ausrüstung

The new, experimental steel helmet for the airborne infantry (note army decal). Later, all paratroopers of the Wehrmacht wore the Luftwaffe paratrooper helmet.
Der neue Fallschirmspringerhelm der Fallschirminfanterie. Er wurde später ersetzt durch den Springerhelm der Luftwaffe.

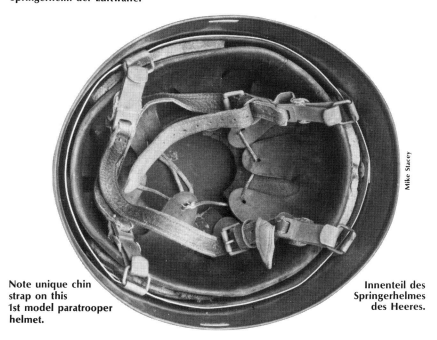

Mike Stacey

Note unique chin strap on this 1st model paratrooper helmet.

Innenteil des Springerhelmes des Heeres.

George Petersen

2nd model paratrooper helmet with army decals and spanner bolts.

Springerhelm der Luftwaffe, jedoch mit dem Heeresadler auf der linken Seite.

1st model paratrooper helmet with 2nd style national emblem decal (Luftwaffe).

1. Modell des Springerhelmes mit neuer Art Luftwaffenadler.

1st model paratrooper helmet with 1st style national emblem decal (Luftwaffe).

1. Modell des Springerhelmes mit alter Art Luftwaffenadler.

Ludwig Baer

George Petersen

1st model jump smock with exposed zippers in wear. Note army breast eagle and belt buckle.

1. Modell der Springerkombination des Heeres.

2nd model, green smock.

2. Modell der Springer-kombination.

2nd model step-in smock with Luftwaffe breast eagle.

"Knochensack" mit Luftwaffenadler.

Eric Queen

George Petersen

1st model.
1. Modell.

2nd model.
2. Modell.

Left: K98 ammunition bandoleer, 1st model.
Links: Munitionsbandolier für die K98 Munition, 1. Modell.

57

Long version. Ausführung lang.

Paratrooper gloves, light model.
Die Fallschirmspringerhandschuhe.

Short
version.
Ausführung kurz.

Protective gloves worn during airborne landings.
Handschuhe schützen den Springer bei der Landung.

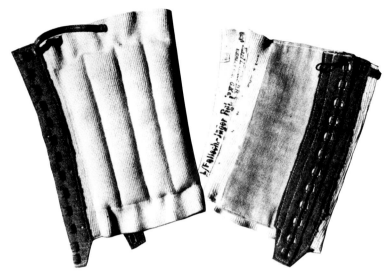

1st model knee pads which were worn under the special paratrooper trousers.
Knieschoner, 1. Modell. Diese wurden unter der speziellen Springerhose getragen.

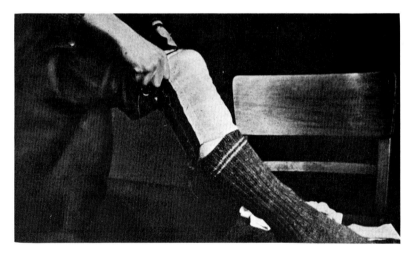

2nd model knee pads which were worn over the paratrooper trousers.
Knieschoner, 2. Modell. Diese wurden über der Hose getragen.

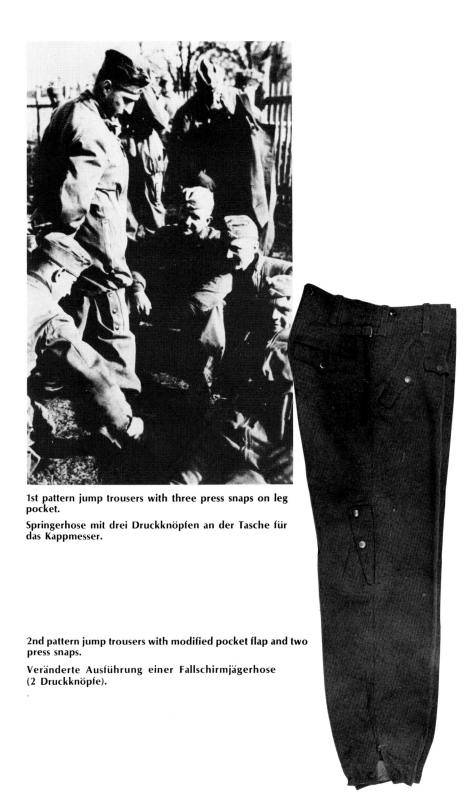

1st pattern jump trousers with three press snaps on leg pocket.

Springerhose mit drei Druckknöpfen an der Tasche für das Kappmesser.

2nd pattern jump trousers with modified pocket flap and two press snaps.

Veränderte Ausführung einer Fallschirmjägerhose (2 Druckknöpfe).

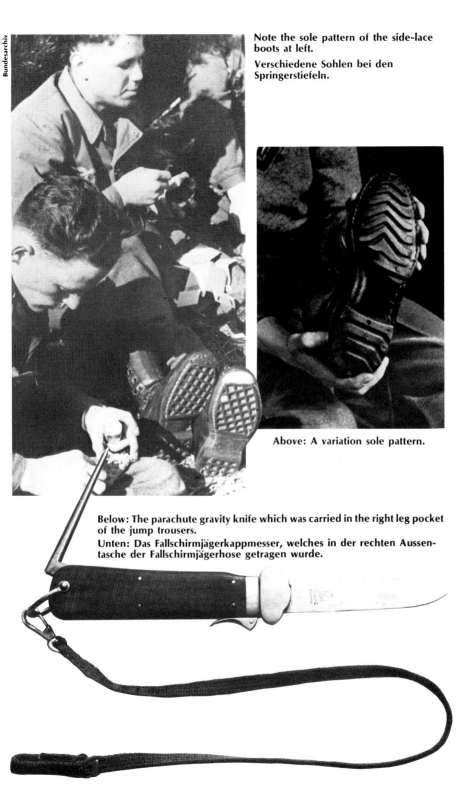

Note the sole pattern of the side-lace boots at left.

Verschiedene Sohlen bei den Springerstiefeln.

Above: A variation sole pattern.

Below: The parachute gravity knife which was carried in the right leg pocket of the jump trousers.
Unten: Das Fallschirmjägerkappmesser, welches in der rechten Aussentasche der Fallschirmjägerhose getragen wurde.

61

Airborne Training

Fallschirmsprungausbildung

On January 29, 1936, Hermann Göring, in his capacity as head of the Luftwaffe, ordered the institution of a parachute school at Stendal, located west of Berlin. The first parachute training class was begun only after very thorough testing of special jump clothing and equipment between May 4 and July 3 of 1936.

One year later, the army also began jump training at Stendal for its volunteer officers and NCOs of the new Army Airborne Infantry Company (Fallschirm-Infantrie Kompanie). This unit used the identical training procedures and equipment as the Luftwaffe.

Gemäss Befehl des "Reichsministers der Luftwaffe und Oberbefehlshabers der Luftwaffe" wurde ab dem 29.01.1936 am Fliegerhorst in Stendal-Borstel die Fallschirmschule Stendal von der Luftwaffe aufgebaut. Nach eingehender Erprobung der Sprungbekleidung der Fallschirmjägers und der Ausbildungstechnik wurde vom 04.05. bis 03.07.1936 der erste Lehrgang für Fallschirmspringer durchgeführt. Erst ein Jahr später begann in Stendal das Heer mit der Sprungausbildung seiner Offiziere und Unteroffiziere, die zur Fallschirminfanterie-Kompanie gehörten und sich freiwillig zu dieser Truppengattung gemeldet hatten. Sie nutzten die gleichen Ausbildungsverfahren

Stendal, the Albrecht the Bear barracks.
Stendal, die Albrecht der Bär Kaserne.

Initially, ground training consisted of the forward and backward fall and rolls, putting on and removing the parachute harness, gathering the parachute together in front of a wind machine, and exercises on the "hanger." Only after four weeks of individual and "stick" jump training on the ground did the first real jump take place. After completing ground training and before the actual in-flight jumps, every embryo paratrooper was taught to pack the RZ-1 parachute.

To acquire the Army Parachute badge, a total of six jumps had to be made. The first and second were individual jumps from a height of about 200 meters, the third was a group of "stick" jump without weapons from a height of 120 meters, the fourth was a dusk or night jump also from 120 meters, the fifth was again a "stick" jump without weapons from 120 meters, and the sixth was tactical jump in platoon strength without weapons, again from 120 meters.

The army's parachute jump training was carried out exclusively at the Luftwaffe parachute school at Stendal until the integration with the Luftwaffe units in January 1939.

The Army Parachute badge was worn officially until December 31, 1938, when it was exchanged for that of the Luftwaffe. It should be noted that many former army parachutists continued to wear their badge as a symbol of pride in their membership in the former Army Airborne Infantry Company.

---

und die gleichen Ausbildungseinrichtungen wie die Fallschirmjäger-Kameraden von der Luftwaffe. So stand zunächst die Bodenausbildung mit dem Vorwärts- und Rückwärtsfall und der Rolle vorwärts und rückwärts im Dienstplan, dann folgte Ausbildung im An- und Ablegen des Gurtzeuges, Bergen und Einfangen des Fallschirmes sowie Übungen an der Aufhängevorrichtung. Erst wenn die Ausbildung im Verhalten beim Einzel- und Reihensprung abgeschlossen war, folgte nach rund vierwöchiger Ausbildung der eigentliche Sprungdienst. Zum Erwerb des begehrten Fallschirmschützenabzeichens mussten insgesamt 6 Absprünge erfolgreich absolviert werden: 1. und 2. Sprung waren Einzelsprünge aus ca. 200 Meter Höhe, der 3. Sprung war ein Reihensprung ohne Waffe, aus 120 Meter Höhe, der 4. ein Dämmerungs- oder Nachtsprung, ebenfalls aus 120 Meter Sprunghöhe, der 5. wieder ein Reihensprung ohne Waffe aus 120 Meter. Der letzte Sprung war ein taktischer Sprung im Zugrahmen ohne Waffe aus 120 Meter Höhe.

Noch vor dem Sprungdienst wurde die Ausbildung im Packen des Fallschirmes vom Typ R.Z. 1 durchgeführt, so dass jeder Fallschirmspringer auch ein Fallschirmpacker war. Die Fallschirmsprungausbildung des Heeres wurde bis zur Eingliederung in die Fallschirmtruppe der Luftwaffe ausschliesslich an der Fallschirmschule der Luftwaffe durchgeführt. Das Fallschirmschützenabzeichen des Heeres wurde offiziell bis zum 31.12.1938 getragen, ab dem 01.01.1939 war es gegen das Fallschirmschützenabzeichen der Luftwaffe auszutauschen. Trotz dieser Anweisung trugen weiterhin viele Fallschirminfanteristen ihr altes Heeresfallschirmschützenabzeichen.

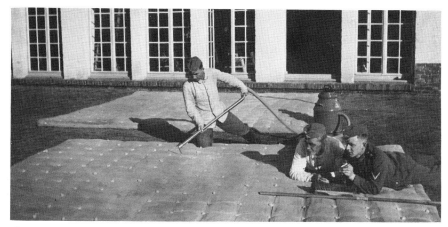

The "mat", an important feature in the training of forward and backward falls.
Die "Bodenmatte," wichtig für die Ausbildung im Vorwärts- und Rückwärtsfall.

Forward roll.
Rolle vorwärts.

Backward roll.
Rolle rückwärts.

Flying roll.
Flugrolle.

Forward roll - without the mat!
"Vorwärtsfall" - ohne Bodenmatte!

Backward roll. The training hall at the Luftwaffe parachute school in Stendal is in the background.
Rückwärtsfall. Im Hintergrund die Ausbildungshalle der Fallschirmschule in Stendal.

Learning to put on the harness of the RZ-1 parachute.
Erlernen des Anlegens des Gurtzeugs zum Fallschirm RZ-1.

A simulated training jump out of the door.
Sprung von der Übungsleiter: kurz vor dem
Absprung!

The jump.
Der Absprung.

Standing at the door of a Ju-52 on the ground.
Übungssprung aus dem am Boden stehenden Flugzeug.

Leaving the aircraft.
Absprung.

Jumping into a safety net, which as a training practice during the war. This photo was taken at Dreux, France in 1941, where an airborne training facility was located.

Einzelsprung aus einer Attrappe in das Sprungtuch. Diese Art der Ausbildung erfolgte im Krieg. Hier ein Bild von der Fallschirmsprungausbildung in Dreux, Frankreich 1941.

Training on the hanger.

Ausbildung an der Hänge-vorrichtung.

A necessary, but unpopular training exercise. The paratrooper must get on his feet as quickly as possible to avoid being dragged by his parachute.

"Windesel": Erlernen des schnellen Aufstehens nach der Landung.

The "wind machine."

Der "Windesel" bei der Arbeit.

Packing the RZ-1 parachute (R-Rücken/back, Z-Zwangsauslösung/automatic opening, 1-first model).
Fallschirmpackausbildung am RZ-1.

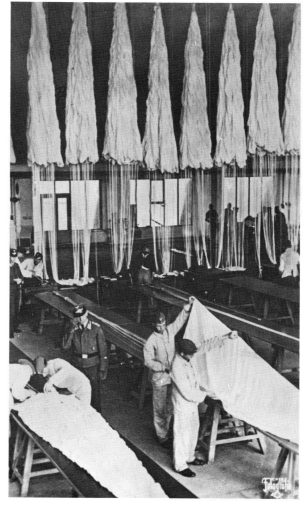

Laying out the canopy.
Legen der Fallschirm-bahnen.

Checking and putting the lines in order.
Ordnen der Fangleinen.

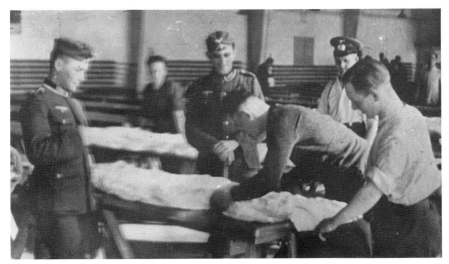

Putting the canopy into the bag (left: Oberjäger Fugmann, killed in Holland in 1940.
Verpacken der Fallschirmkappe in den Verpackungssack (links: Oberjäger Fugmann, gefallen 1940 in Holland).

Putting the lines into the parachute bag.
Einschlaufen der Fangleinen und Verpacken.

Packing the parachute with the help of the Luftwaffe.
Fallschirmpackausbildung - mit Hilfe der Luftwaffe.

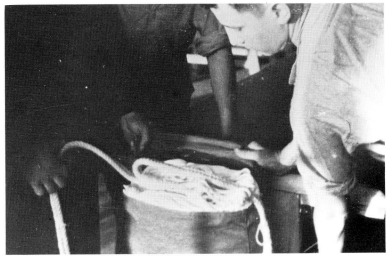

Packing the static line.
Einschlaufen der Fangleinen
und der Aufziehleine.

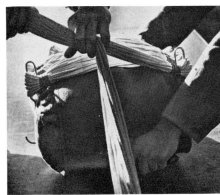

Nearly ready!
Abschluss der Arbeit.

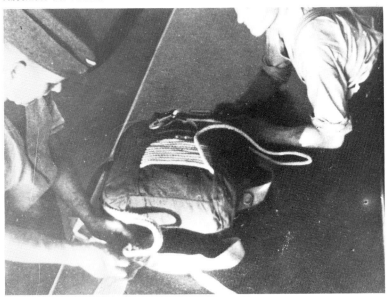

Ju-52 cargo carrier of the Luftwaffe airborne school.
Transportflugzeug Ju-52 der Fallschirmschule.

Before jump training, airborne infantry soldiers took a flight to acquaint themselves with the aircraft and the feeling of flight.

In Friedenszeiten erfolgte vor dem Sprungdienst ein "Gewöhnungsflug" für die Fallschirminfanteristen, da die meisten noch nie ein Flugzeug von innen gesehen hatten.

Jump training: Checking the RZ-1 parachute. Note that at this early time the airborne infantry jumped without steel helmets. Right: Lt. Haedrich, fourth from right, Lt. Stangenberg.

Sprungdienst: Überprüfen des Gurtzeuges (beachte: Die Sprungausbildung erfolgte noch ohne Springerhelm). Rechts: Lt. Haedrich, vierter von rechts: Lt. Stangenberg.

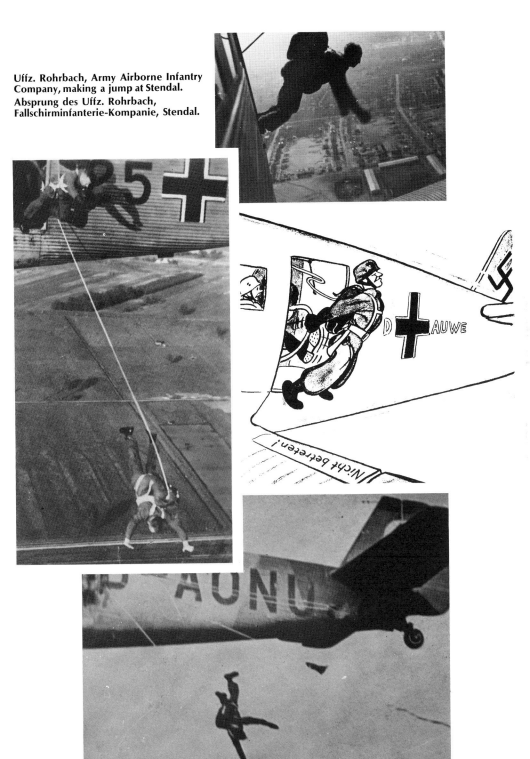

Uffz. Rohrbach, Army Airborne Infantry
Company, making a jump at Stendal.
Absprung des Uffz. Rohrbach,
Fallschirminfanterie-Kompanie, Stendal.

The parachute opens.
Der Fallschirm öffnet sich.

Airborne infantry of the Abn. Inf. Bn.
which carried the tradition of Assault
Battalion No. 7.
Fallschirmschützen des Fallschirm-Inf.-
Btl. - Träger der Tradition des Sturmbtl.
Nr. 7.

A good landing!
Glückliche Landung.

Not exactly the best landing!
Nicht gerade ein schulmässiger Landefall!

Of immediate importance is to get on one's feet as soon as possible.
Umlaufen des Fallschirms, um ein Schleifen durch das Gelände zu vermeiden.

After the jump the RZ-1 parachutes are hung up to dry.
Fallschirme werden zum Trocknen hoch gezogen.

Note two different styles of jump trousers (two and three flap snaps on the side pocket for the paratrooper knife), and the 1st model jump smock with Luftwaffe national emblem.
Man beachte die unterschiedlichen Springerhosen (2 und 3 Druckknöpfe für die Kappmessertasche) und das 1. Modell der Springerkombi mit dem Luftwaffenadler.

A mass jump.
Reihensprung.

Above: Tactical mass jump with weapons containers.
Oben: Taktischer Sprung in Zugstärke mit
Waffenbehälter.

The Airborne Infantry Company 1937-1938

Die Fallschirminfanteriekompanie 1937-1938

The first jump course for the army airborne infantry from May 4 - June 3, 1937. Left to right: Hübner, Hasseldick, Pagels, Gröger, Massalsky, Vogel, Stab, Geisler, Loos, Straehler-Pohl (later a Knight's Cross holder), Cording, Deiters, Stangenberg, Haertel, Becker, Haedrich and Rogge.

Der 1. Springerlehrgang für das Heer vom 04.05. - 03.06.1937. Von links nach rechts: Hübner, Hasseldick, Pagels, Gröger, Massalsky, Vogel, Stab, Geisler, Loos, Straehler-Pohl (später Ritterkreuzträger), Cording, Deiters, Stangenberg, Haertel, Becker, Haedrich, Rogge.

NCOs and men of the army airborne company during the second jump course.

Unteroffiziere und Mannschaften der Fallschirminfanterie-Kompanie, die am 2. Springerlehrgang teilnahmen.

Lt. Pagels and Uffz. Büttner (note the sleeve stripe on the jump smock designating a lieutenant, and the chevron on the collar designating an NCO.

Lt. Pagels und Unteroffizier Büttner (beachte das Dienstgradabzeichen des Leutnants an der Springerkombination und des Unteroffiziers-Winkel am Kragen).

Ready for a jump: (left to right) OGefr. Emil Rüssmann, Gefr. Max Blum, and Lt. Pagels.

Fertig zum Sprung: (von links nach rechts) OGefr. Emil Rüssmann, Gefr. Max Blum, Lt. Pagels.

Last instructions. Uffz. K. Welter
and Olt. Pelz (center).
Einweisung in den Sprungdienst.
Uffz. K. Welter und Olt. Pelz
(mitte).

An airborne infantry squad standing by a Ju-52 transport.
Eine Fallschirminfanteriegruppe zum Sprungdienst vor der Ju-52 angetreten.

Putting on the RZ-1 harness.
Anlegen des Sprungfallschirmes
RZ-1.

Proud airborne infantrymen!
Stolze Fallschirminfanteristen!

Receiving the Army Paratrooper Badge from Hptm. Zahn.
Verleihung der Fallschirmschützenabzeichen durch Hptm. Zahn.

Army Paratrooper Badge,
heavy version.
Fallschirmschützenabzeichen
des Heeres, schwere
Ausführung.

Document for the Army Parachute Badge, serial number 21.
Verleihungsurkunde zum Fallschirmschützenabzeichen Nr. 21.

Left to right: Fw. Knacke, Lt. Haertel, Lt. Stangenberg, and Fw. Walter Schmidt.

Von links nach rechts: Fw. Knacke, Lt. Haertel, Lt. Stangenberg, Fw. Walter Schmidt.

89

Winter maneuvers, September 20, 1937. Hptm. Zahn (center) and Lt. Pelz (right).
Herbstmanöver, 20.09.1937. Hptm. Zahn (mitte) und Lt. Pelz (rechts).

The first Sergeant-Major ("Spiess") of the Army Airborne Infantry Company, HFw. Emil Preikschat.
Der 1. Kompaniefeldwebel ("Spiess") der Fallschirm-Infanterie-Kompanie, HFw. Emil Preikschat.

Winter maneuvers.
Herbstmanöver.

An army parachute license with a note that Gefr. H. Mordhorst was transferred to the 5th Company, Parachute Regiment 1, on January 1, 1939.

Der Heeresfallschirmschützenschein mit der Eintragung, dass mit Wirkung zum 01.01.1939 der Gefr. H. Mordhorst zur 5./Fallschirmjägerregiment 1 versetzt worden ist.

"Seppl," the airborne dog belonging to Olt. Pelz.

Auch das gab es bei der FIK: Der fallschirmspringende Dackel des Olt. Pelz.

91

Between heaven and earth!
Sicher der Erde entgegen!

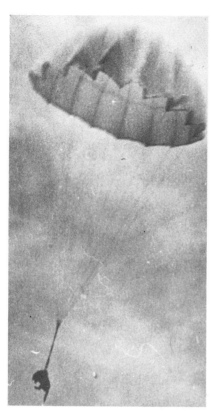

A good landing with the help of a blanket.
Mit Hilfe einer Decke gut gelandet!

Infantry training in Elm, spring 1938.
Geländedienst in Elm, Frühjahr 1938.

Last bugle call for the airborne infantry company.
"Das Ganze halt!"

THE ARMY AIRBORNE INFANTRY BATTALION

DAS FALLSCHIRMINFANTERIEBATAILLON

*The F.I.B. was instituted by an order dated March 15, 1938 (in Allgemeine Heeresmitteilungen 1938, No. 286), effective June 1, 1938.
*Das F.I.B. wurde mit einer Verfügung vom 15.3.1938 (in Allgemeine Heeresmitteilungen 1938, Nr. 286) m.W.v. 1.6.1938 aufgestellt.

When the Airborne Infantry Company was expanded to a battalion, a wide range of activities was created by the Ist Battalion commander which included the specialized training of new personnel. Heidrich wrote: "We acquired young officers and excellent other ranks and now the grist mill began to operate. Together, we worked diligently because we were a new branch striving for recognition and acceptance. Initially, I made the mistake of wanting to educate the troopers according to current, strict and dogmatic infantry training methods. Because of the uniqueness of this new branch, I soon realized that I had to let the men develop their own individuality and techniques. During the training I tended to confront the men with crisis situations and required their maximum efforts.

We were aware that in our special situation, our lives often hung by a hair and that the act of collective jumping created a special relationship between officer, NCO and men. We were different from other troops. The paratroopers were members of the most dangerous branch of service during peacetime, comparable only to the mountain troops."

Mit Vergrösserung der F.I.K. zum Fallschirminfanterie-Bataillon (F.I.B.) tat sich für den ersten Bataillonskommandeur ein weites Betätigungsfeld auf: Ausbildung der Personalergänzung. Major Heidrich schrieb dazu: "Wir erhielten frische, junge Offiziere und junge, ausgezeichnete Mannschaften. Jetzt begann die Schleifmaschine zu arbeiten. Wiederum arbeiteten wir fleissig. Wir waren eine junge Truppe, die nach Anerkennung strebte...Ich beging zunächst den Fehler, dass ich diese neue Truppe streng in meinem, ich möchte sagen, doktrinär-dogmatischen Infanteriegeist erziehen wollte. Diese junge Truppe aber hatte zu viel Blut, sie sträubte sich dagegen. Bald erkannte ich, dass man diese Truppe sich in ihrem eigenen Geist entwickeln lassen müsse. Man schaltete allmählich um auf etwas ähnliches wie Reitergeist. Kurz um, überall Frische und Initiative. In der Ausbildung stellte ich die Truppe grundsätzlich vor Krisenlagen und verlangte von ihr höchste Anstrengung...Wir waren uns halt bewusst, dass unser Leben oft an einem dünnen Strick hängt. Das Sprungerlebnis schaffte ein besonderes, kameradschaftliches Verhältnis zwischen Offizier, Unteroffizier und Mann. Es

Stendal, the home of the Army Airborne Infantry Battalion.
Stendal, Standort des Fallschirminfanterie-Bataillons.

The commander,
Major Richard Heidrich.
Der Kommandeur,
Major Richard Heidrich.

Lt. Otto Heckel (here, wearing a Luftwaffe uniform with army paratrooper badge) became adjutant to the battalion commander. He was later promoted to colonel in the General Staff but served under Heidrich through 1945.
Lt. Otto Heckel (hier in Luftwaffenuniform und u.a. mit dem Heeresfallschirmschützenabzeichen dekoriert) wurde Adjutant des Btl. Kdr. Er war mit Heidrich bis zum Kriegsende eng verbunden.

95

Officers of the Army Airborne Infantry Battalion. Left to right: Lt. Krüger, Lt. Stangenberg, Lt. Straehler-Pohl and Lt. Haertel.
Offiziere des Fallschirminfanteriebataillons. Von links nach rechts: Lt. Krüger, Lt. Stangenberg, Lt. Straehler-Pohl, Lt. Haertel.

June 1, 1938, the establishment of the Army Airborne Infantry Battalion.
01.06.1938 - Aufstellung des Fallschirminfanteriebataillons.

The battalion jumped on the island of Borkum during a naval fleet maneouver on June 21/22, 1938.

Teilnahme am Flottenmanöver der Marine vom 21.-22.06.1938, dabei Fallschirmabsprung auf die Insel Borkum.

The battalion commander also jumped.
Auch der Bataillonskommandeur springt.

On guard.
Sicherung.

Going home by island railroad.
Rückmarsch per Inselbahn.

Marching to field training.
Marsch zum
Gefechtsdienst.

The Airborne Infantry Battalion, under the command of Major Heidrich, took over the traditions of Assault Battalion No. 7.
Das FIB übernahm unter Major Heidrich die Tradition des Sturmbataillons Nr. 7.

The 1st Company after a training jump, summer 1938. At far left is Fw. Lips, next to him Olt. Bückel (killed in Holland, 1940), and at far right is Fw. Mensch (killed in Poland, 1939).
1. Kompanie nach dem Sprungdienst, Sommer 1938. Vorne links: Fw. Lips, daneben Olt. Bückel (gefallen in Holland 1940), hinten rechts: Fw. Mensch (gefallen in Polen 1939).

The 1st Company after jump training.
Die 1. Kompanie nach dem Sprungdienst.

A harbor tour in Hamburg by battalion NCOs on August 31, 1938.
Hafenrundfahrt der Unteroffiziere am 31.08.1938 in Hamburg.

Major Heidrich also demanded thorough infantry training with numerous excercises to supplement the specialized jump training and eventually achieved the high levels of proficiency reached by the old Assault Battalion No. 7. Constant tactical training and a heightened level of realistic and vigorous training paid off.

The training schedule was expanded with more jump training, long distance marches, tank and locomotive driving, all of which were designed to permit the paratrooper to meet and cope with any combat situation.

The battalion had three companies, as well as an engineer and signal platoon. The short-term conscripts were dismissed and sent into the reserves, leaving a well-tempered and trained battalion of airborne infantry.

---

unterschied sich grundsätzlich von anderen Truppen. Das kam daher, dass die Fallschirmtruppe im Frieden eben die gefährlichste Truppe war, von der schon im Frieden der Einsatz auf Tod und Leben verlangt wurde. Vergleichbar damit war nur noch in gewissem Sinne die Hochgebirgstruppe.''

Major Heidrich war es auch, der besonders eine vielseitige, infanteristische Ausbildung mit vielen Übungen und Übungsplatzaufenthalten befahl und - wie im Traditionstruppenteil, dem Sturmbataillon Nr. 7 - durch ständige, taktische Schulung und äusserste Härte einen ausgesprochen hohen Ausbildungsstand erreichte. Sprungausbildung, Fahren von Panzern, LKW's, ja sogar Eisenbahn, sowie Fussmärsche über grosse Entfernungen und Sprungdienste gehörten zum Ausbildungsplan. Wenngleich das Bataillon Oktober 1938 auch zunächst über nur 3 Kompanien sowie Pionier- und Nachrichten-Zug verfügte und die ersten Reservisten entliess, war das Bataillon durchweg hervorragend infanteristisch ausgebildet.

Another maneuver!
Wieder Manöver!

Airborne infantrymen.
Fallschirminfanterie.

Army Paratrooper Badge of Gefr. Esche, with the inscription
"Airborne Inf. Bn".
Heeresfallschirmschützenabzeichen des Gefr. Esche mit der
Gravur "Fallschirm-Inf.-Btl".

Commander of the 1st Company, Obl.
Freiherr von Brandes.
Kompaniechef der 1. Kompanie, Obl.
Freiherr von Brandes.

(Below) Major Heidrich and his adju-
tant, Lt. Heckel, during a short break.
Note the regimental band in the
background.
(Unten) Major Heidrich und sein
Adjutant Lt. Heckel bei einer
Marschpause. Im Hintergrund der Rgt.-
Spielmannszug.

103

Airborne infantrymen must be able to fulfill all missions, including demolition.
Pionierausbildung am Mittellandkanal 1938.
Fallschirminfanteristen müssen alles können!

Range shooting in the Goslar training area, 1938.
Schiessausbildung in Goslar, 1938.

Many VIPs visit the Army Airborne Infantry Battalion, a sign that a conflict is expected.
Besuch und Inspizierung - erste Anzeichen für bevorstehende Einsätze, Herbst 1938.

Pre-War Employment

Einsatz im Frieden

The battalion's first employment was under the 7th Flying Division when they participated in the occupation of the Sudetenland. There was no shooting during "Operation Green" and the mission was carried out like air transport training from October 7 to October 17, 1938. The success of this air transport maneuver was carefully observed by the Supreme Command of the Wehrmacht (OKW), which decided that all paratroopers must, in the following year, become a part of the Luftwaffe. The sole exception to this was the army's 22nd Infantry Division (LL, Air Assault).

Der erste Einsatz im Rahmen der 7. Fliegerdivision stand bevor: Die Besetzung des Sudetenlandes. Obwohl der militärische Einsatz im scharfen Schuss entfiel, wurde das Unternehmen "Grün" als Lufttransportübung vom 07.10. bis 17.10.1938 manövermässig durchgeführt.

Der Erfolg dieser Übung war für die oberste Wehrmachtsführung so überzeugend, dass das OKW eine für das F.I.B. folgenschwere Entscheidung fällte: Alle Fallschirmjäger und Fallschirminfanteristen sollten ab 1939 zur Luftwaffe gehören, Luftlandetruppen (das war die 22. Inf. Div.) sollten dagegen beim Heer verbleiben.

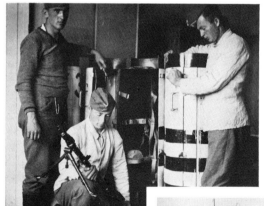

Preparing for the first mission with the 7th Flying Division. The objective was the airfield at Freudenthal. The weapons' containers are packed and loaded.
Vorbereiten des Einsatzes zur Besetzung des Sudetenlandes im Rahmen der 7. Fliegerdivision. Einsatzraum Freudenthal. Beladen der Waffenbehälter.

The Airborne Infantry Battalion is air transported in about 250 Ju-52s.
Lufttransport des FIB im Rahmen der 7. Fliegerdivision mit insgesamt ca. 250 Ju-52.

Freudenthal.

Crash Landing!
Keine gute Landung!

Airborne infantrymen shortly before the occupation of the Sudetenland.
Fallschirminfanteristen kurz vor dem Sudeteneinsatz.

Freudenthal.

Portions of the border fortifications.
Teile der Grenzbefestigungen.

Fortresses and Bunkers in the Freudenthal area.
Bunker und Grenzbefestigung.

A company commander and "Spiess".
Kompaniechef und "Spiess."

Captured without a fight.
Kampflos genommene
Grenzbefestigungen.

General Student visits the airborne infantry.
General Student bei den Fallschirmschützen.

A group photo near Freudenthal.
Das Erinnerungsphoto.

Another bunker
system at
Zwoggau.
Weitere Bunker-
systeme in
Zwoggau.

111

After a successful mission. Front row, second from left: Lt. Stangenberg.

Nach dem Einsatz. Zweiter von links, vorne: Lt. Stangenberg.

Hptm. Prager has three sleeve stripes. Lt. Stangenberg is to his left.
Mit drei Streifen: Hptm. Prager, daneben Lt. Stangenberg.

OFFICERS/OFFIZIERE

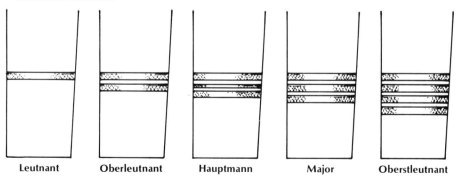

| Leutnant | Oberleutnant | Hauptmann | Major | Oberstleutnant |

NCOs/UNTEROFFIZIERE

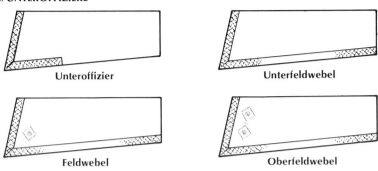

Unteroffizier

Unterfeldwebel

Feldwebel

Oberfeldwebel

Note: The above rank insignia was introduced on June 10, 1938.
Diese Dienstgradabzeichen des FIB wurden am 10. Juni 1938 eingeführt.

Consequently, on January 1, 1939, the Airborne Infantry Battalion was officially transferred from the army to the Luftwaffe as the IInd Battalion/Parachute Regiment 1. Previously, the battalion had been transferred from its old garrison at Stendal to Wolfenbüttel near Brunswick and was stationed at the Roselies Barracks. When this occured, part of the 2nd Company, on February 4, 1938, jumped into the barracks area under bad weather conditions.

The Airborne Infantry Battalion received its army motorized battalion standard from the Inspector of the Infantry, Generalmajor Ott, on November 4, 1938, and officially took over the traditions of the Assault Battalion No. 7. Major Heidrich was transferred to the staff of the 7th Flying Division in Berlin at this time, and Captain Prager took over command of the battalion. With this, the history of the army's airborne infantry came to an end. General Student's revolutionary concepts of using the airborne force in a strategic role, deep in the enemy's rear, had come into being.

Somit folgte ab 01.01.1939 der Wechsel des F.I.B. vom Heer zur Luftwaffe als II. Bataillon Fallschirmjägerregiment 1. Zuvor aber verlegte das Bataillon vom alten Standort Stendal nach Braunschweig/Wolfenbüttel in die Roselies-Kaserne. Bei dieser Gelegenheit sprangen bei böigem Wetter Teile der 2. Kompanie am 04.02.1938 in die Kaserne. Das Fallschirminfanterie-Bataillon bekam in feierlicher Form vom Inspekteur der Infanterie, Generalmajor Ott, ihre Heeresstandarte und übernahm offiziell die Tradition des Sturmbataillons Nr. 7. Das Bataillon übernahm nun Hauptmann Prager, Major Heidrich ging zum Stab der 7. Fliegerdivision nach Berlin.

Damit endete die Entwicklung der Fallschirminfanterie beim Heer. Die Luftwaffe und die revolutionären Vorstellungen des General Kurt Student, die Fallschirmtruppe selbständig und operativ weit vor den vordersten Heeresteilen einzusetzen, hatten sich durchgesetzt.

Farewell to Stendal.
Abschied von Stendal.

The lion on the Burg square, one of the symbols of Brunswick.
Der Löwe auf dem Burgplatz, eines der Wahrzeichen der Stadt Braunschweig.

The new home of the Airborne Infantry Battalion: Brunswick, Roselies barracks.
Der neue Standort des FIB: Braunschweig, Roselies-Kaserne.

November 4, 1938. Decorated for the arriving Airborne Infantry Battalion.
04.11.1938. Festlich geschmückte Kaserne - das Fallschirminfanterie-Bataillon rückt ein.

The new standard of the Airborne Infantry Battalion.
Die neue Standarte des FIB.

November 4, 1938. The Inspector of Infantry, Generalmajor Ott, presents the new infantry standard to Major Heidrich.

04.11.1938: Übergabe der neuen Standarte durch den Inspekteur der Infanterie, Generalmajor Ott, an Major Heidrich.

Parading for General der Flieger Felmy, Generalmajor Behlendorf, and the battalion commander, Major Heidrich.

Vorbeimarsch am General der Flieger Felmy, dem Standortältesten, Generalmajor Behlendorf, und dem Btl. Kdr., Major Heidrich.

Major Heidrich, Oberbürger-
meister Dr. Hesse, General der
Flieger Felmy, Generalmajor
Behlendorf.

Airborne infantry (note the
army and Luftwaffe helmet
decals).
Fallschirminfanteristen.

A spiked helmet and paratrooper helmet, living traditions within the Wehrmacht of 1938!
Pickelhaube und Springerhelm - lebende Tradition in der Wehrmacht 1938!

Marching into the Roselies barracks.
Einmarsch in die Roselies-Kaserne.

Changing of the guard.
Wachwechsel.

After taking over the Roselies barracks, the battalion commander, Major Heidrich, reviews the companies.
Nach Übernahme der Roselies-Kaserne. Der Btl. Kdr., Major Heidrich, schreitet die Front ab.

Some paratroopers take over the barracks by jumping into the area.
Einige Soldaten erreichten die neue Roselies-Kaserne per Fallschirm.

After a successful landing inside the Roselies barracks area.
Nach der glücklichen Landung in der Roselies-Kaserne.

The battalion is subject to numerous visits and inspections at its new home in Brunswick. Here, General Student speaks with soldiers of the battalion. Hptm. Prager is at right.

Auch im neuen Standort reissen die Besuche und Inspizierungen nicht ab. Hier ist General Student beim FIB zu Besuch. Rechts: Hptm. Prager.

The airborne infantry and its equipment on display for interested visitors.
Vorführung vor interessierten Heeresoffizieren.

Lt. Witzig presents his engineer platoon to high ranking military and political leaders.
Lt. Witzig stellt seinen Pionierzug hohen militärischen und politischen Führern vor.

The 1st Company. ▶
Die 1. Kompanie.

Hptm. Prager and a squad of airborne infantrymen.
Hptm. Prager und eine Gruppe Fallschirminfanteristen.

An airborne infantry squad
with machine guns, K98s,
Bergmann machine pistols and
various personal equipment.

Die Fallschirminfanterie-
gruppe, ausgerüstet
mit dem leichten MG, der
Bergmann MPi und dem K98.

Note the different types of weapons and equipment carried by a squad. At far right: Glössner.
Eine Vielzahl von Handwaffen und persönlicher Ausrüstung. Ganz rechts: Glössner.

The last days of the Airborne Infantry Battalion. At left: Schütze W. Scholten.
Die Tage der Heeres-Fallschirminfanterie sind gezählt! Links: Schütze W. Scholten.

Christmas celebration, 1938.
Weihnachtsfeier 1938.

Der Führer und Reichskanzler

hat aus Anlaß der Wiedervereinigung
Österreichs mit dem Deutschen Reich

dem Schützen

Franz Einberger

4. Kompanie, Fallschirm-Infanterie-Bataillon

die
**Medaille zur Erinnerung
an den 13. März 1938**
verliehen.

Berlin, den 23. Januar 1939

**Der Staatsminister
und Chef der Präsidialkanzlei
des Führers und Reichskanzlers**

Meissner

This document was presented to F. Einberger by the Abn. Inf. Bn., although the battalion did not take part in the Austrian occupation.

Diese Urkunde wurde von dem Fallschirm-Infanterie-Bataillon ausgestellt, obgleich das Btl. selbst nicht an der Österreich-Besetzung teilgenommen hatte, wohl aber der Schütze F. Einberger.

THE IInd BATTALION/PARACHUTE REGIMENT 1

DAS II. BATAILLON/FALLSCHIRMJÄGERREGIMENT 1

In Peace and War

Im Frieden und Krieg

With the battalion's integration into the Luftwaffe, the 7th Flying Division grew in size and strength. The battalion's visable differences were the blue-grey uniform of the Luftwaffe and the green "Fallschirmjäger-Rgt. 1" cuff title. Although the 7th Flying Division was not combat ready, it had to make itself available for the occupation of Czechoslovakia. The division, including II/Parachute Rgt. 1, was deployed from March 14 to March 20, being airlifted into the area around Prague, already occupied by army units. Through political means, a shooting war had once again been averted.

Although the fledgling German paratroopers had played a strategic role in the Czech occupation, its existance was relatively unknown to the German public. This changed, however, when the battalion participated in the great parade in Berlin on April 20, 1939, to honor Hitler's 50th birthday and

Mit Eingliederung in die Luftwaffe, die äusserlich sichtbar wurde durch die Luftwaffenuniform mit dem grünen Regimentsärmelstreifen, wuchs nun ständig die 7. Fliegerdivision. Obgleich noch nicht fertig aufgestellt, hatte sie bald einen weiteren Einsatz zu bestehen: Die Restbesetzung der Tschechoslowakei. Auch hier konnte letztendlich der scharfe Schuss politisch verhindert werden, doch kam die Division, und damit das II./FJR 1 vom 14.03. bis 20.03.1939 zum Einsatz. Wieder war es nur ein Lufttransport in den Raum um Prag, der vorher bereits von Heeresverbänden besetzt worden war.

Obgleich die junge deutsche Fallschirmtruppe militärisch bei der Tschecheibesetzung schon eine wichtige und strategische Rolle spielte, war ihr Vorhandensein in der Öffentlichkeit noch relativ unbekannt. Das änderte sich durch die Teilnahme an der grossen "Führerparade" am 20.04.1939 und anlässlich der Parade für den Prinzregenten Paul von Jugoslawien am 20.06.1939 in Berlin. Die neue Truppengattung mit ihrer eigenartigen

Hptm. Prager, the commander of the IInd Bn./Parachute Rgt. 1.

Hptm. Prager, der ab dem 01.01.1939 das unbenannte und dem Fallschirmjägerregiment 1 unterstellte II. Btl. übernahm.

Above: The Parachute Regiment 1 cuff title (top: for officers, and bottom: for NCOs and enlisted ranks).

Oben: Der Ärmelstreifen des Fallschirmjäger-Regimentes 1 (oben: für Offiziere, unten: für Unteroffiziere und Mannschaften).

Unteroffizier Klein wears the Fallschirmjäger-Regiment 1 cuff title on his army tunic.

Unteroffizier Klein in Parade-Heeresuniform mit dem Luftwaffen-Ärmelstreifen Fallschirmjäger-Regiment 1.

127

The uniform transition from the Army Airborne Battalion to FJR 1. Feldwebel Dr. Tietjen is at right.

Heeres- und Luftwaffenuniformen im FJR 1.

Lt. Straehler-Pohl, Hptm. Prager.

Officers of II./FJR 1, some wearing sleeve ranks of the army (left) and some of the Luftwaffe (right) on their jump smocks.

Offiziere des II./FJR 1 - in Heeresuniform, teilweise jedoch mit Dienstgradabzeichen des Heeres (links ein Lt.) und der Luftwaffe (rechts Olt.)

Olt. Pagels, killed in action on Crete on
May 20, 1941.
Olt. Pagels, gefallen am 20.05.1941 auf
Kreta.

Lt. Schwarzmann, a sports teacher who was a winner of three gold medals in the 1936 olympic
games. He was a platoon leader in the 8th Company.
Lt. Schwarzmann, Sportlehrer, dreifacher
Goldmedaillengewinner von 1936. Lt. und
Zugführer in der 8. Kp.

Below: Hptm. Prager and Olt. Böhmler.
Unten: Hptm. Prager und Obt. Böhmler.

The new Luftwaffe uniform with the
regimental cuff title and Army
Paratrooper Badge.
Ein Fallschirmjägerunteroffizier in
Luftwaffenuniform, mit dem
Regiments-Ärmelstreifen und dem
Heeresfallschirmschützenabzeichen.

Prince Regent Paul of Jugoslavia during his state visit to Berlin on June 20 of the same year. On these occasions, their new uniforms and equipment coupled with the perfectly disciplined marching, created great excitement among the spectators.

The battalion utilized the few months of peace remaining before the outbreak of war in September to continue their special training projects in a series of excercises held at different training areas.

Bekleidung und ihrer aussergewöhnlichen Marschdisziplin wurde von der Bevölkerung mit Jubel und Beifall bedacht.

Die Zeit bis zum Kriegsbeginn nutzte das Bataillon für zahlreiche Übungen, Ausbildungsvorhaben und Truppenübungsplatzaufenthalte.

Gefr. Mordhorst wears the old-style jump smock with Luftwaffe breast eagle.
Die "alte" Springerkombination mit dem "neuen" Luftwaffenadler. Gefr. Mordhorst.

The new jump smock.
Die neue Springerkombination.

Left: Oberjäger Trimborn, right: Oberjäger Klein.
Links: Oberjäger Trimborn, rechts: Oberjäger Klein.

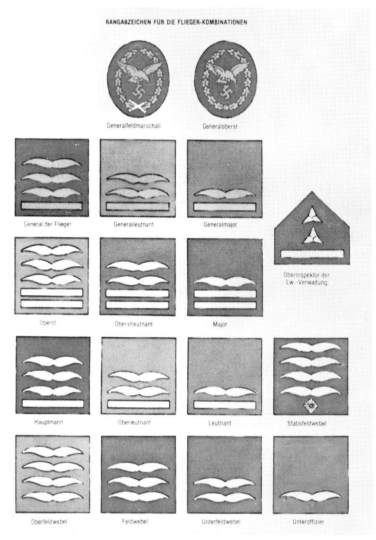

Generalfeldmarschall

Generaloberst

General der Flieger

Generalleutnant

Generalmajor

Oberinspektor der
Lw.-Verwaltung

Oberst

Oberstleutnant

Major

Hauptmann

Oberleutnant

Leutnant

Stabsfeldwebel

Oberfeldwebel

Feldwebel

Unterfeldwebel

Unteroffizier

Luftwaffe sleeve rank insignia for use on flying clothing and the paratrooper jump smock.

Rangabzeichen der Flieger und Fallschirmjäger an ihren Kombinationen.

132

Prague: March 15-23, 1939
Prag: 15.03.1939 - 23.03.1939

The second
Sudetenland mission.
Der 2. Sudetenland
Einsatz.

II./FJR 1 waiting to depart in Burg, near Magdeburg.
Das II./FJR 1 in Bereitschaft in Burg bei Magdeburg.

Formation flight to Prague.
Verbandsflug nach Prag.

Inside a Ju-52 inflight to Prague: 7th Company, 5th Squad (at right is Sanitäter Oppermann, a medical soldier).
In der Ju-52 im Flug nach Prag: 7.Kompanie, 5.Gruppe (rechts: Sanitäter Oppermann).

Above: Just before the parade in Prague. Left: Officers of the II./FJR 1 still wearing army uniforms.
Oben: Vor der Parade in Prag. Links: Die Offiziere des II./FJR 1 noch immer in Heeresuniform!

An interesting mixture of army and Luftwaffe uniforms. Front left: HFw. Hess, 8th Company, 2nd from left: Fw. Rohrbach, and 3rd from left: Uffz. Welter.

Eine bunte Mischung von Heeres- und Luftwaffenuniformen. Vorne: HFw. Hess, 8.Kp., 2. von links: Fw. Rohrbach, 3. von links: Uffz. Welter.

Lt. Trebes (left), the battalion commander, Hptm. Prager (right), and his adjutant, Lt. Heckel (middle).

Der Adjutant und sein Kommandeur: Lt. Heckel (Mitte), Hptm. Prager (rechts) und Lt. Trebes (links).

The parade in Prague.
Die Parade in Prag.

A sightseeing tour. Left to right: Uffz. Haselhorst, Gonscherowski, Schmidt, Herzbach and Obj. Mordhorst.

Ausgang und Stadtbummel. Von links nach rechts: Uffz. Haselhorst, Gonscherowski, Schmidt, Herzbach und Obj. Mordhorst.

Im Namen
des Führers und Obersten Befehlshabers der Wehrmacht
verleihe ich

dem Oberjäger Fritz R e n t z s c h

die Medaille zur Erinnerung an den 1. Oktober 1938
~~mit Spange~~*

Berlin, den 20. Juni 1939.

Für die Richtigkeit:

(Siegel)

(Name, Dienstgrad und Dienststellung)
Hauptmann u. Bataillonskommandeur
* Bei Nichtverleihung streichen.

Nr. 1922   /39 B

Der Kommandeur
der Flieger-Division 7

Student
Generalmajor

Award document for the Commemorative Medal of October 1, 1938.
Urkunde für die Medaille zur Erinnerung an den 1. Oktober 1938.

Im Namen
des Führers und Obersten Befehlshabers der Wehrmacht
verleihe ich

dem   Gefreiten Franz E i n b e r g e r

die Medaille zur Erinnerung an den 1. Oktober 1938
mit Spange*

Berlin, den 20. Juni 1939.

Für die Richtigkeit:

(Siegel)

(Name, Dienstgrad und Dienststellung)
Hauptmann u. Bataillonskommandeur
* Bei Nichtverleihung streichen.

Nr.   1735/3 9 A

Der Kommandeur
der Flieger-Division 7

Student
Generalmajor

Award document for the Commemorative Medal of October 1, 1938 with the "Prague Castle" bar.
Urkunde für die Medaille zur Erinnerung an den 1. Oktober 1938 mit Spange "Prager Burg."

"Prague Castle" bar.
Spange "Prager Burg."

April 1939 - August 1939

Rehersal inside the Roselies barracks for the Führer's birthday parade in Berlin on April 20, 1939.
Vorüben der grossen Berlin-Parade in der Roselies-Kaserne.

Berlin, April 20, 1939.
Berlin, 20.04.1939.

Sanssouci.

The parade in Berlin, April 20, 1939.
Die Parade am 20.04.1939 in Berlin.

The next parade in which the battalion participated was on June 20, 1939 for Prince Paul of Jugoslavia. Again, the II./FJR 1 was applauded by the Berlin population.
Parade am 20.06.1939 anlässlich des Prinzregenten Paul von Jugoslawien. Wieder war das II./FJR 1 dabei!

ril 20, 1939.
.04.1939.

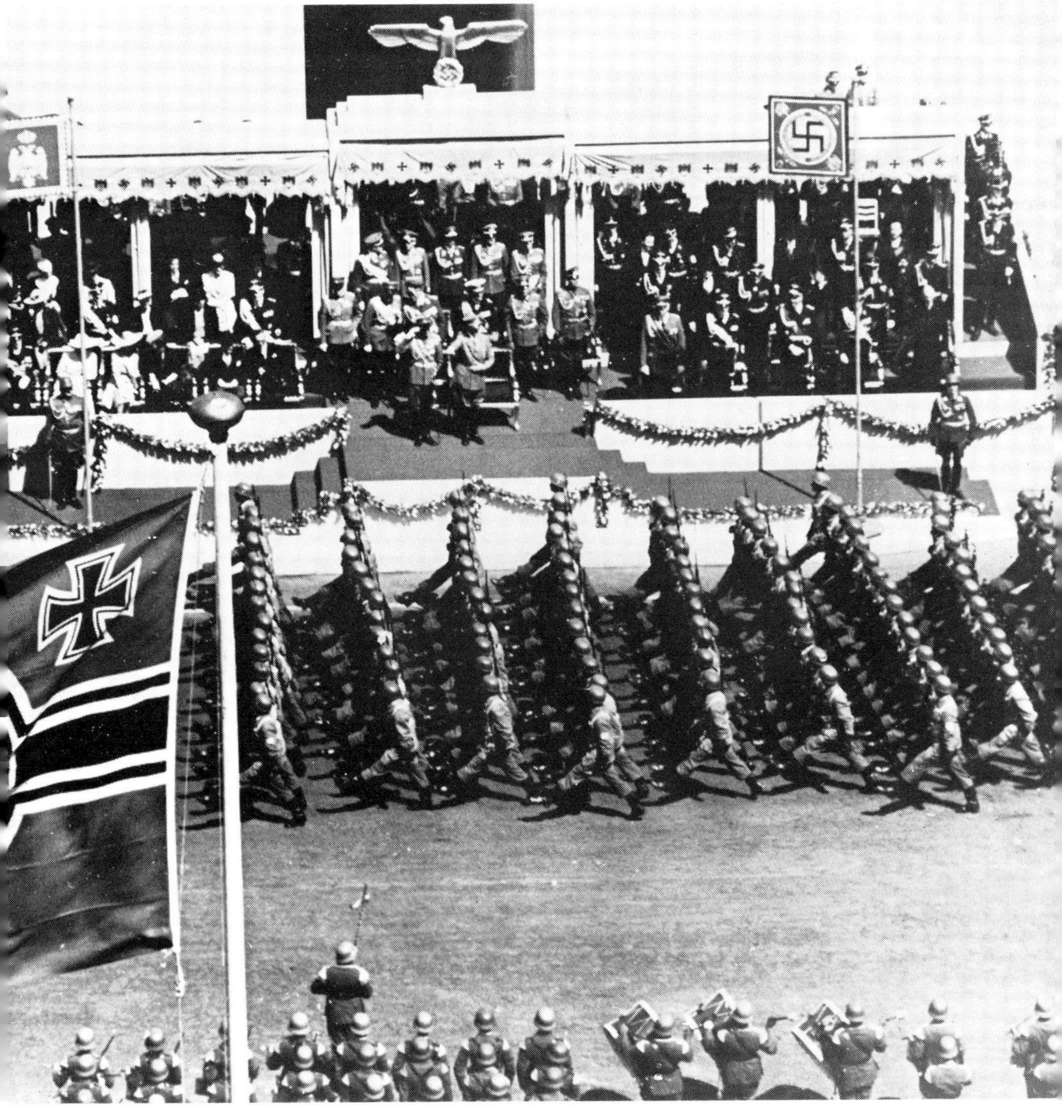

At the Hammerstein training area, July 5-12, 1939. Lt. Straehler-Pohl is at right.

Das II./FJR 1 auf dem Truppenübungsplatz Hammerstein, 05.07.-12.07.1939. Rechts: Lt. Straehler-Pohl.

The drivers of the II./FJR 1 displaying various weapons.

Kraftfahrer des II./FJR 1 auf dem Truppenübungsplatz Hammerstein, 05.07-12.07.1939.

A break during the training in Hammerstein.

Marschpause. Truppenübungsplatz Hammerstein.

Training area Bergen. Note the army parachute badge.

Truppenübungsplatz Bergen. Beachte das Heeresfallschirmschützenabzeichen.

Hptm. Prager giving orders to his staff at Bergen on July 28, 1939.

Befehlsausgabe: Der Kommandeur, Hptm. Prager, auf dem Truppenübungsplatz Bergen, 28.07.1939.

Crossing a river by raft.
Übersetzen über Gewässer mit Behelfsmitteln.

Another training area, this time at Wildflecken from August 2-15, 1939.

Und wieder geht es zum Truppenübungsplatz Wildflecken: 02.08.-15.08.1939.

The 5th Company marches through
the camp at Wildflecken.
Marsch der 5. Kompanie im Lager
Wildflecken.

Critical comments.
Abschlussbesprechung.

Terrain tour, Wasserkuppe, August 1939. Hptm. Prager is third from left.
Besprechung auf der Wasserkuppe (3. von links: Hptm. Prager).

Poland: September 1-24, 1939

Polen: 01.09.1939-24.09.1939

On August 30, 1939, the battalion was put on alert, their arms containers were packed, and the JU52 transports were loaded. However, the rapid advances of German ground forces deep into Polish territory negated the use of paratroopers and most of their projected missions were cancelled. Their only combat engagements were at the airport at Ulenz and, two days later, at Wola Gulowska. This battle left eight dead and thirteen wounded. These actions, resulting in unnecessary casualties, led to a vehement argument between Heidrich and Student. Heidrich was so disgusted with the misuse of his airborne troops as standard infantry that he returned to the army and took over command of a reserve infantry regiment.

Am 30.08.1939 wurde das Bataillon alarmiert; die Sprungbehälter wurden gepackt, die JU-52 beladen. Der 2. Weltkrieg hatte begonnen!

Das Angriffstempo des Heeres mit Unterstützung durch die Luftwaffe war jedoch so gross, dass dieser "Blitzkrieg" der Fallschirmtruppe keine Chance zum Einsatz gab. Mehrere geplante Aufträge entfielen. Lediglich die Besetzung des Flugplatzes Ulenz und das anschliessende Gefecht bei Wola Gulowska, bei der das Bataillon 8 Tote und 13 Verwundete hatte, forderte die Fallschirmjäger. Diese Kämpfe und die daraus entstandenen unnötigen Opfer führten zu Auseinandersetzungen zwischen Heidrich und General Student, so dass Heidrich zum Heer zurückkehrte und ein Reserve-Infanterie-Regiment als Kommandeur übernahm.

Preparing for war on Schönfeld airfield, near Liegnitz.
Vorbereitungen auf dem Flugplatz Schönfeld bei Liegnitz.

Special identification card for flying personnel and paratroopers.
Sonderausweis für Flieger- und Fallschirmtruppe.

The old and new Sergeant-Major ("Spiess"): Fw. Knacke and OFw. Schmidt (right).
Der alte und der neue "Spiess": Fw. Knacke und OFw. Schmidt (rechts).

6th Company: Lt. Gayer and Lt. Dick.
6.Kompanie: Lt. Gayer und Lt. Dick.

Commanders get
hungry too! Hptm.
Prager.
Auch Komman-
deure haben
Hunger! Hptm.
Prager.

Listening to the Wehrmacht radio report: Hptm. Prager (third from left), to his left is Lt. Krüger, seventh is R. Müller, eighth is Fw. Mensch and ninth is W. Müller.
Gespannt verfolgt man den Wehrmachtsbericht: Hptm. Prager (3. von links), daneben vorne Lt. Krüger, 7. R. Müller, 8. Fw. Mensch, 9. W. Müller.

The II./FJR 1 follows the army in trucks with the hope of getting a mission. Note Hptm. Prager still wears his army uniform.

Per LKW geht es weiter nach Osten. Das II./FJR 1 folgt dem Heer mit der Hoffnung, doch noch zu einem Sprungeinsatz zu kommen.

Radom.

Waiting and playing
"skat."
Warten und Zeitver-
treiben.

Tactical orders finally arrive by Fieseler Storch. The battalion is to take the Vistula bridge at Pulawy by a combat jump.

Per Fieseler Storch kommt ein taktischer Auftrag: Der Weichsel-Brücke bei Pulawy durch Sprungeinsatz.

The orders are given by the battalion commander, Hptm. Prager.
Befehlsausgabe durch den Btl. Kdr., Hptm. Prager.

Below: The Vistula bridge at Pulawy. The army advanced too quick and got there first!
Unten: Die Weichsel-Brücke bei Pulawy. Das Heer war schneller!

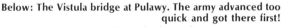

After the army had taken the bridge, the paratroopers could only visit the lightly damaged bridge as tourists.

Nach Nehmen der Brücke durch das Heer blieb den Fallschirmjägern nur die friedensmässige Besichtigung der teilweise zerstörten Brücke.

The Ulenz airfield was taken on September 21, 1939.
Flugplatz Ulenz, am 21.09.1939 genommen.

On guard at the Ulenz airfield.
Wache am Flugplatz Ulenz.

General Student visits the IInd Battalion at
Ulenz.
General Student kommt!

The first dead enemy soldiers.
Die ersten Toten.

The first Polish POWs.
Die ersten polnischen Gefangenen.

Burial of dead Polish soldiers.
Bestattung polnischer
Gefallener.

Moving eastward on September
23, 1939.
Es geht weiter nach Osten,
23.09.1939.

157

More Polish POWs.
Weitere polnische
Soldaten werden
Gefangene.

A short rest.
Kurze Rast.

Lt. Stangenberg.
Paratroopers
become light
cavalry!
Lt. Stangenberg.
Fallschirmjäger
können auch
reiten!

Above: Wola
Gulowska, the first
real battle on Sep-
tember 24.
Oben: Wola
Gulowska, die
erste Feuertaufe,
24.09.1939.

159

Combat!
Kampf!

Where is the enemy? At right: Oberjäger Fugmann.
Wo ist der Feind? Rechts: Oberjäger Fugmann.

160

Engaged with a Polish artillery regiment.
Im Kampf gegen ein polnisches Artillerie Regiment.

The first cemetery of the II./FJR 1.
Der erste Soldatenfriedhof des II./FJR 1.

Fw. Mensch, one of the first to be killed in action, September 24, 1939.
Einer der ersten Gefallenen der deutschen Fallschirmtruppe: Fw. Mensch.

The first cemetery of the paratroopers within the walls of the Polish fortress at Deblin.
Beisetzung der gefallenen Fallschirmjäger auf dem alten Fort der Festung Deblin.

The first paratrooper cemetery of World War II - many more of which would follow!
Der erste Soldatenfriedhof der Fallschirmtruppe im 2. Weltkrieg - noch viele, viele sollten folgen!

After the battles in Poland.
Im Ruhequartier nach dem Polenfeldzug.

Going back to Germany by truck.
Im Kfz.-Marsch zurück.

Crossing the Vistula.
Über die Weichsel.

Grenade-launcher squad of the 8th Company on their way to Brunswick via
Tschenstochau-Radomsko-Oppeln, in mid-October.
Granatwerfergruppe der 8. Kp., II./FJR 1 auf dem Marsch über Tschenstochau nach Radomsko,
von dort Mitte Oktober über Oppeln in den Standort.

The spirit of an elite troop - "Chamberlain! We're coming!"

Der Geist der Fallschirmtruppe - nach dem Sieg über Polen!

After the Polish campaign, Major Heidrich takes leave from his old battalion. He then took command of an army infantry regiment. He would later return to be the first commander of Parachute Regiment 3.

Nach dem Polenfeldzug verabschiedet sich Major Heidrich, um beim Heer als Regimentskommandeur ein Reserve Infanterie Regiment zu übernehmen. Er später der erste Regimentskommandeur des FJR 3 werden!

The commander of the 7th Flying Division, General Student, greets the II./FJR 1 in Brunswick-Broitzen, on October 13, 1939. Behind him is the battalion commander, Hptm. Prager.

Der Kommandeur der 7. Fliegerdivision, General Student, begrüsst das II./FJR 1 in Braunschweig-Broitzen nach dem Polenfeldzug am 13.10.1939.

Hptm. Prager, the first paratrooper to get the Iron Cross 2nd Class.
Verleihung des E.K. II an den Kommandeur des II./FJR 1, Hptm. Prager.

More Iron Crosses: Olt. Böhmler, OFw. Rohrbach.
Weitere EK - Verleihung durch General Student: Olt. Böhmler, OFw. Rohrbach.

168

One of the earliest Iron Cross 2nd Class award documents given to a paratrooper. OFw. W. Rohrbach was the platoon leader of the signal platoon, II./FJR 1.

Verleihungsurkunde zum EKII.

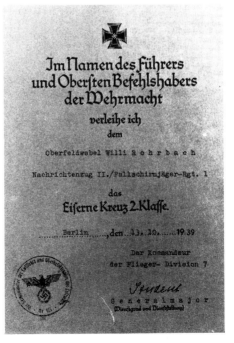

Im Namen des Führers und Obersten Befehlshabers der Wehrmacht

verleihe ich

dem

Oberfeldwebel Willi R o h r b a c h

Nachrichtenzug II./Fallschirmjäger-Rgt. 1

das

Eiserne Kreuz 2. Klasse.

Berlin ,den 11. 10. 19. 39

Der Kommandeur
der Flieger- Division 7

Student

G e n e r a l m a j o r
(Dienstgrad und Dienststellung)

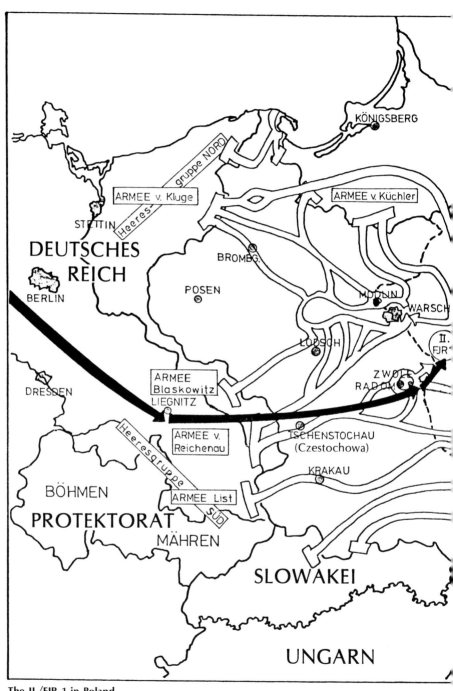

KÖNIGSBERG

gruppe NORD

ARMEE v. Kluge

ARMEE v. Küchler

STETTIN

Heeres-

**DEUTSCHES
REICH**

BERLIN

BROMBG.

POSEN

MODLIN

WARSCH

LODSCH

II.
FJR

DRESDEN

ARMEE
Blaskowitz

LIEGNITZ

ZWOL
RADOM

ARMEE v.
Reichenau

Heeresgruppe

TSCHENSTOCHAU
(Czestochowa)

BÖHMEN

ARMEE List

SÜD

KRAKAU

PROTEKTORAT

MÄHREN

SLOWAKEI

UNGARN

The II./FJR 1 in Poland.
Das II./FJR 1 im Polenfeldzug.

UEN

UNION DER
SOZIALISTISCHEN
SOWIET-
REPUBLIKEN

RUSSLAND

LEMBERG

ROMÄNIEN

Brunswick: October 1939 - May 1940

Braunschweig: Oktober 1939 - Mai 1940

After the fall of Poland, the II/Parachute Rgt. 1 returned to Wolfenbüttel via Radomsko-Czestochowa-Oppeln where they continued their training. This consisted of ski training in the Harz mountains in conjunction with the army's 22nd Infantry Division (Air Assault) and using live ammunition in their exercises.

Only after a theoretical war game at the Ministry of Aviation on March 4, 1940, was it decided that the airborne units should get an important mission in the upcoming Western campaign...the breaching of Fortress Holland.

Nach Ende des Polenfeldzuges kehrte das II./FJR 1 über Radomsko - Tschenstochau - Oppeln nach Wolfenbüttel zurück. Die vielseitige Ausbildung der ehem. Heeresinfanteristen wurde fortgesetzt: Skiausbildung im Harz, Gefechtsdienst im scharfen Schuss und Beladeübungen zusammen mit der 22. Inf. Div. (LL) des Heeres. Erst das Planspiel beim Luftfahrtministerium am 04.03.1940 zeigte den Offizieren, dass die Fallschirmtruppe für den Frankreichfeldzug eine entscheidende Rolle zufallen sollte: Das Öffnen der Festung Holland!

Christmas 1939.
Weihnachten 1939.

Brunswick-Broitzen in early 1940. Note the knee pads, gloves and gas mask bag worn under the jump smock.
Braunschweig-Broitzen Anfang 1940.

Fw. Hörig at far left, beside him is
Fw. Kühne.
Fw. Hörig, links, daneben Fw. Kühne.

The special gas mask bag
for paratroopers.
Gasmaskenbeutel.

173

Jump training, 1940.
Sprungausbildung, 1940.

The Parachute Badge of the Luftwaffe.
Das Fallschirmschützenabzeichen der Luftwaffe.

Verleihungsurkunde

Ich verleihe dem

Gefreiten Jakob S t e f a n i

das Abzeichen für

Fallschirmschützen

Berlin, den 4.Dezember 193 9

Der Reichsminister der Luftfahrt
und Oberbefehlshaber der Luftwaffe

I. A.

[signature]
Generalmajor

Nr. 1352 /39

Gefr. Jakob Stefani's award document for the paratrooper badge.
Urkunde für das Fallschirmschützenabzeichen.

Ausbildungsübersicht
für
I. Fallschirmgrundausbildung — II. Unterführerausbildung — III. Ausbildung zum Absetzleitenden

Ausbildungsziel	Ausbildungsdauer	Ausbildungsgebiete	Teilnehmer	Voraussetzung für die Teilnahme
1	2	3	4	5
		I. Fallschirmgrundausbildung		
Truppenverwendungsfähiger Fallschirmschütze	a) **Friedensausbildung** 7½ Wochen	**Zu a) Theoretisch:** Geschichte und Entwicklung des Fallschirmes „Der Fallschirm R. Z. 1" und andere Baumuster. Unterricht über Erste Hilfe. Fliegerischer und wetterkundlicher Unterricht (nur zur Einweisung). Verhalten beim Absprung. Aufgaben und Einsatzmöglichkeiten der Fallschirmtruppe (Offz.Unterricht). **Praktisch:** Körperliche Schulung: Bodenübungen, Übungen an der Aufhängevorrichtung, Schleifübungen, Absprünge von der Übungsleiter. Vorübungen für Einzel und Reihenabsprung. An und Ablegen des Gurtzeuges. Frühsport, Sportspiele, Marschübungen, Übungen an den Waffenbehältern, Waffenausbildung. Packen des Fallschirmes R. Z. 1, Packen unter besonderen Verhältnissen. Einweisungsflüge. Durchführung von 6 Pflichtsprüngen, davon 1 Dämmerungs oder Nachtsprung und 1 Absprung mit anschließender Schulschießübung. Theoretische und praktische Prüfung.	Springendes Personal der Fallschirmtruppe	1. Freiwilligkeit 2. Fallschirmtauglichkeit 3. Psychologische Eignung.
	b) **Verkürzte Friedensausbildung** 6½ Wochen	**Zu b) Theoretisch:** Geschichte und Entwicklung des Fallschirmes „Der Fallschirm R. Z. 1" und andere Baumuster. Unterricht über Erste Hilfe. Fliegerischer und wetterkundlicher Unterricht (nur zur Einweisung). Verhalten beim Absprung. **Praktisch:** wie unter a), jedoch ohne Waffenausbildung.		
	c) **Kriegsausbildung** 4 Wochen	**Zu c) Theoretisch:** Geschichte und Entwicklung des Fallschirmes „Der Fallschirm R. Z. 1" und andere Baumuster. Unterricht über Erste Hilfe. Verhalten beim Absprung.		

Ausbildungsziel	Ausbildungsdauer	Ausbildungsgebiete	Teilnehmer	Voraussetzung für die Teilnahme
1	2	3	4	5
		Zu c) Praktisch: Körperliche Schulung, Bodenübungen, Übungen an der Aufhängevorrichtung, Schleifübungen, Absprünge von der Übungsleiter, Vorübungen für Einzel und Reihenabsprung. An und Ablegen des Gurtzeuges. Frühsport. Packen des Fallschirmes R. Z. 1. Packen unter besonderen Verhältnissen. Einweisungsflug, Durchführung von 6 Pflichtabsprüngen, davon 1 Dämmerungs oder Nachtabsprung und 1 Absprung mit anschließender Schulschießübung.		
Voll verwendungsfähiger Unterführer der Fallschirmtruppe und Fallschirmwart für Sprungfallschirme	6 Wochen	**II. Unterführerausbildung** Vertiefung des bei der Fallschirmgrundausbildung erlernten Stoffgebietes. Unterweisung in den Lehr und Ausbildungsmethoden der Schule. Lösung von selbständigen Aufgaben im Ausbildungs und Wartungsdienst. Erteilung von Unterricht über Fallschirme, Leitung von vorbereitenden Übungen, Ausbildung am Waffenbehälter, Beaufsichtigung beim Packen von Fallschirmen. Prüfung von Anzug, Gurtzeug und Anbringung des Fallschirmes. Überwachung des Absprunges. Einweisung über das Verhalten beim Absprung. Einweisung in den Absetzdienst. Fallschirmwartausbildung für Sprungfallschirme.	Offiziere, Unteroffiziere und Unteroffizieranwärter der Fallschirmtruppe	Abgeschlossene Fallschirmgrundausbildung
Befähigung zum selbständigen Absetzen von Fallschirmeinheiten	2 Wochen	**III. Ausbildung zum Absetzleitenden** Beurteilung von Absetzplätzen: a) theoretisch nach Karte und Luftbild, b) praktisch durch Augenbeobachtung. Anflugübungen für den Fallschirmabsprung, Absetzübungen mit Puppen aus verschiedenen Höhen für Einzel und Reihenabsprung und für Absprung aus der Kette; selbständiges Absetzen von Fallschirmschützen und Fallschirmeinheiten.	Unterführer der Fallschirmtruppe	Abgeschlossene Unterführerausbildung an der Fallschirmschule

Stoffverteilungsplan für Fallschirmgrundausbildung

Lfd. Nr.	Lehrfach	Friedensausbildung 7½ Wochen Unterricht	Prakt. Ausbild.	Verkürzte Friedensausbildung 6½ Wochen Unterricht	Prakt. Ausbild.	Kriegsausbildung 4 Wochen Unterricht	Prakt. Ausbild.
1	Wetterkunde	5		5		—	
2	Flugzeugortung	2		1		—	
3	Flugdienstsicherheitsbestimmungen	3		3		1	
4	Flugzeugkunde	2		2		—	
5	Fluglehre	2		2		—	
6	Reichsluftwaffe	2		—		—	
7	Erste Hilfe	4		4		3	
8	Verhalten beim Absprung	5		5		4	
9	Aufgaben der Fallschirmtruppe	2		—		1	
10	Fallschirmgeschichte	2		2		—	
11	Fallschirmbaumuster	2		2		1	
12	R. Z. 1	20		20		15	
13	36 D. S. 28	4		2		—	
14	27 II. S. 20	2		2		—	
15	30 I/II S. 24	3		1		—	
16	Unterricht am Flugzeug	1		1		1	
17	Anlegen des Gurtzeuges		6		4		3
18	Bergen der Fallschirme		6		4		2
19	Bodenübungen		16		15		12
20	Übungen an der Aufhängevorrichtung		16		15		12
21	Praktische Übungen an der Ju. 52		16		15		12
22	Einfangen des Schirmes		9		7		6
23	Packübungen R. Z. 1		88		88		60
24	Packen unter besonderen Verhältnissen		8		8		8
25	Übungen an den Waffenbehältern		2		2		—
26	Waffenausbildung		21		—		—
27	Sportspiele bzw. Schwimmen		14		12		—
28	Marschübungen		10		6		—
29	Einweisungsflüge		2		2		1
30	Sprungdienst		26		26		18
31	Prüfungen		8		8		—
	Zusammen Unterricht und Prakt. Ausbildung	61	248	52	212	26	134
	Insgesamt (Stunden)	309		264		160	

Anlage 2

Training plan for fundamental parachute training, 1940.
Stoff- und Ausbildungsplan, 1940.

Paratroopers must be able to do anything, including skiing! Soldiers of the II./FJR 1 on their way to the Harz.
Fallschirmjäger müssen alles können - auch Skilaufen! Soldaten des II./FJR 1 auf dem Weg zur Skiausbildung in den Harz.

Hptm. Prager.

Combat training on skis.
Gefechtsausbildung auf Skiern.

The battalion staff and signal platoon. In center: Lt. Haedrich, to his left: OFw. Rohrbach.
Stab und Nachrichten-Zug II./FJR 1. Mitte: Lt. Haedrich, daneben OFw. Rohrbach.

The 5th Company in Altenau/Harz. Olt. Schwarzmann is at right with civilian hat and clothes.
He was a sports teacher, gold medal winner at the 1936 olympic games, and later a Knight's
Cross holder (1940).
Skiausbildung der 5. Kp. in Altenau/Harz. Rechts mit Hut und in Zivil: Der Sportlehrer,
mehrfacher Olympiasieger von 1936 und späterer Ritterkreuzträger, Olt. Schwarzmann.

Training with much snow and fun!
Winterkampf - mit viel Schnee und Spass!

"Day of the Wehrmacht" in Brunswick, March 15, 1940.
"Tag der Wehrmacht" in Braunschweig, 15.03.1940.

The NCOs and officers of the 6th Company in Werl, the day before the Moerdijk mission, May 9, 1940. The company commander is Olt. Stangenberg.
Das Uffz.-Korps der 6.Kp., II./FJR 1 in Werl, am 09.05.1940, dem Vortag vor dem Hollandeinsatz. Kp. Chef ist Olt. Stangenberg.

Werl, shortly before the campaign in Holland.
Nach dem Sport und unmittelbar vor dem Hollandeinsatz, Soldaten des II./FJR 1.

Holland: May 10 - June 7, 1940

Holland: 10.05.1940 - 07.06.1940

On May 10, 1940, the IInd Battalion took off from Werl at about 4:50am, jumped at 6:00am north and south of the bridges at Moerdijk and within three hours of fierce fighting, controlled them. The battalion, which was behind enemy lines, was subject to fierce counterattacks by the Dutch Army but held its positions to May 12. Their losses amounted to 28 killed and 33 wounded. The battalion commander, Captain Prager, was among the wounded. He, 1st Lieutenants Schwarzmann (also badly wounded) and Tietjen were subsequently awarded the Knight's Cross.

Am 10.05.1940 startete das II. Bataillon gegen 04.50 Uhr von Werl, sprang gegen 06.00 Uhr nördlich und südlich der Strassen- und Eisenbahnbrücken bei Moerdijk ab und nahm schon nach 3 Stunden harter Kämpfe die Objekte. Allein auf sich gestellt hielt das Bataillon die Brücken bis zum 12.05. gegen wütende Gegenangriffe der Holländer. Der Auftrag, die für das Heer wichtigen Übergänge unversehrt zu nehmen und zu halten, wurde glänzend erfüllt, wenngleich das Bataillon wiederum schmerzliche Verluste hatte: 28 Tote, 33 Verwundete und Sprungverletzte waren zu beklagen. Unter den Verwundeten waren auch der Bataillonskommandeur, Hptm. Prager und Olt. Schwarzmann, die zusammen mit dem Lt. Tietjen für diesen Einsatz mit dem Ritterkreuz ausgezeichnet wurden.

The quarters in Werl, the airfield from where the II./FJR 1 took off for Holland.
Die Unterkünfte in Werl, dem Absprungflughafen des II./FJR 1.

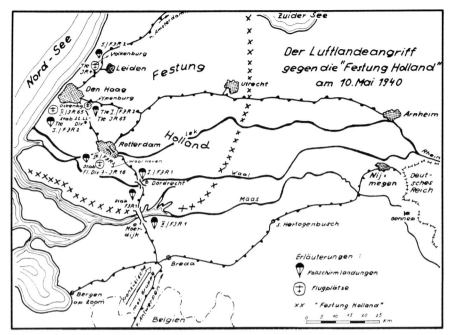

The attack on Holland, May 10, 1940.
Der Angriff gegen Holland, 10.05.1940.

Receiving their final orders.
Letzte Befehle, danach geht es zum Einsatz.

One of the Ju-52s used for the Holland operation.
Eine der Ju-52 Transportflugzeuge für den Hollandeinsatz.

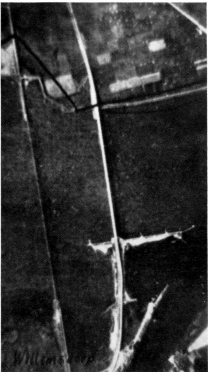

The bridges at Moerdijk.
Die Brücken bei Moerdijk.

The railroad bridge - 1400m long.
Die Eisenbahnbrücke - 1400m lang.

The road bridge - 1200m long.
Die Strassenbrücke - 1200m lang.

Over Holland: a drawing by Baitz, a war artist whose work specialized on the paratroopers.
So sah der PK-Maler der Fallschirmtruppe, Baitz, den Absprung über Holland am 10.05.1940.

The jump and landing.
Absprung und Landung.

The bunker north of the road bridge, taken by Lt. Tiedjen's platoon, 5th Company.
Der Bunker nördlich der Strassenbrücke, gestürmt von der 5. Kp.

A trench system taken by paratroopers, now a battalion command post.
Fallschirmjäger haben das Objekt genommen. Die Unterstände dienen nun als Btl.-
Gefechtsstand.

Uffz. Gabbey (left), Lt. Haedrich (right).
Uffz. Gabbey, links, Lt. Haedrich, rechts.

Lt. Haedrich and OFw. Rohrbach, the signal platoon leader at the battalion command post.
Lt. Haedrich, OFw. Rohrbach, der Nachrichtenzugführer des Btl. auf dem Gefechtsstand.

After bitter fighting against Dutch counterattacks.
Die ersten, harten Kämpfe sind vorbei.

Machine gun position of the 7th Company.
MG-Stellung der 7. Kompanie.

Anti-tank weapon of the 7th
Company.
Panzerbüchse der 7. Kp. in
Stellung.

Defense positions of the 7th and
8th Companies, south of the
Moerdijk bridges.
Einsatzräume der 7. und 8. Kp.,
südlich der Moerdijk-Brücken.

Reconnaissance.
Spähtrupp der 7. Kompanie.

Position of the 6th Company.
Stellung der 6. Kompanie.

Dutch prisoners of war.
Holländische Kriegsgefangene.

Waiting for the Panzers.
Warten auf die Einsatztruppen des Heeres.

191

The village of Moerdijk.
Moerdijk.

Help yourself! Paratroopers of the 6th Company.
Man muss sich nur zu helfen wissen! Fallschirmjäger der 6. Kompanie.

Captured Dutch light artillery.
Holländische Artillerie.

Company command post, Olt. Pagels.
Kp. Gefechtsstand. Olt. Pagels.

Waiting for the enemy or the Wehrmacht.
Warten.

Resting.
Gefechtspause.

They're coming!
Sie kommen!

They finally come - a reconnaissance vehicle of the 9th Panzer Division, May 12, 1940.
Spähpanzer der 9. Panzerdivision. Endlich!

A happy meeting with the Panzers!
Stürmische Begrüssung!

Contact is made with army units.
Verbindung Heer und Fallschirmtruppe hergestellt.

Cheers!
Begrüssungsschluck.

Meeting with the badly
wounded battalion comman-
der, Hptm. Prager.
Beim verwundeten Btl. Kdr.,
Hptm. Prager.

Hptm. Prager after the Moerdijk battle.
Hptm. Prager nach den harten Kämpfen.

A sketch of Hptm. Prager.
Ein Zeichner hielt diese Szene fort.

The first tanks of the 9th Panzer Division on the road from Lage Zwaluve to Moerdijk.
Die ersten Panzer der 9. Panzerdivision auf der Strasse von Lage Zwaluve nach Moerdijk.

May 12, 1940 at 1500 hours - contact with the 9th Panzer Division.
12.05.1940: 15.00 Uhr - Vereinigung mit schnellen Truppen der 9. Pz.-Div.

A Pz-IV near a bunker at
Hollandsch Diep/Moerdijk.
Bunker am Hollandsch Diep
(Moerdijk). Panzer übernehmen
die Sicherung.

Infantrymen relieve the exhausted
paratroopers.
Eigene Infanterie löst die
erschöpften Fallschirmjäger ab.

199

A group photo: Infantry and paratroopers.
Gruppenphoto: Infanterie und Fallschirmjäger.

The reconnaissance and tank troops are followed by the infantry and artillery.
Nach den Aufklärern und Panzern kamen die Männer der Infanterie und Artillerie.

Hptm. Prager and Olt. Pagels by a knocked-out Dutch Panhard P-178 armored vehicle.

Abgeschlossener holländischer Panzer, dahinter Hptm. Prager und Olt. Pagels.

After the battle one can see the obvious change in their faces. Olt. Straehler-Pohl, Hptm. Prager and Olt. Haedrich.

Nach den Kämpfen - die Strapazen sind in den Gesichtern deutlich zu sehen. Olt. Straehler-Pohl, Hptm. Prager, Olt. Haedrich.

201

The battalion commander and his company commanders/officers of his staff. Left to right: Olt. Pagels, Olt. Pelz, Olt. Straehler-Pohl, Hptm. Prager, Lt. Haedrich, Olt. Böhmler and Olt. Stangenberg.

Der Kdr. und seine Kp. Chefs bzw. Offiziere im Stab. Von links nach rechts: Olt. Pagels, Olt. Pelz, Olt. Straehler-Pohl, Hptm. Prager, Lt. Haedrich, Olt. Böhmler, Olt. Stangenberg.

Olt. Böhmler, Hptm. Prager, Lt. Haedrich.

Not every truck was able to make it to Rotterdamm.

Nicht jedes Fahrzeug schafft es bis Rotterdamm.

Killed in action.
Gefallene Fallschirm-
jäger.

The Moerdijk mission is completed. The army rolls across the bridge.
Vormarsch des Heeres über die Moerdijk-Brücke. Der Auftrag des II./FJR 1 ist erfüllt.

The battalion buried 28 killed-in-action inside a monastary.

In einem Klosterhof bei Moerdijk ist der 2. Soldatenfriedhof des II./FJR 1. Das Bataillon hatte 28 Gefallene, davon 2 Offiziere. Ehrensalut über den Gräbern.

The cemetery in 1940.
Der Friedhof kurz nach den Kämpfen, 1940.

The com-
memorative
stone in
Moerdijk.
Der
Gedenkstein
in Moerdijk,
1940.

In remembrance of Moerdijk.
Erinnerungsphotos.

After Moerdijk, the battalion went to The Haag on May 21, 1940. Left: Lt. Haedrich and his driver, OFw. Rohrbach.
Nach dem Einsatz geht es am 21.05.1940 nach Den Haag. Links: Lt. Haedrich und sein Fahrer, OFw. Rohrbach.

Marching in The Haag, May 21, 1940.
Einmarsch in Den Haag, 21.05.1940.

The 5th Company. In the center is Olt. Straehler-Pohl.
Die 5. Kp. des Olt. Straehler-Pohl, Mitte.

German paratroopers and
the Dutch royal guard.
Fallschirmjäger und
königliche Garde.

Heavy casualties among the Ju-52 cargo carriers. Crashed aircraft in The Haag area.
Enorme Verluste hatten die Transportflieger bei den Kämpfen um Rotterdamm, Waalhaven und
Den Haag.

One of many
destroyed Ju-52s in
Holland.

Eine von vielen zerstörten
Transportmaschinen in
der Festung Holland.

General Milch, Hptm. Prager and Olt. Kerfin (III./FJR 1).
General Milch, Hptm. Prager und Olt. Kerfin (III./FJR 1).

The home-coming parade in Brunswick. Hptm. Prager, who was wounded and unable to walk, rides at the head of his battalion.

Einmarsch in Braunschweig. Hptm. Prager, noch immer schwer verwundet und nicht gehfähig, an der Spitze seines Bataillons.

Receiving the Knight's Cross from Generalfeldmarschall Göring. Left: Oberst Bräuer, beside him, Hptm. Prager.

Ritterkreuz verleihung für den Hollandeinsatz durch Generalfeldmarschall Göring. Links: Oberst Bräuer, daneben Hptm. Prager.

The victors of Moerdijk.
Die Sieger von Moerdijk.

Hptm. Prager, a brave and beloved
soldier.
Hptm. Prager, ein vorbildlicher und
von allen Soldaten geachteter
Vorgesetzter!

Many soldiers receive their Iron
Cross, 1st and 2nd Class.
Der Ordenssegen.

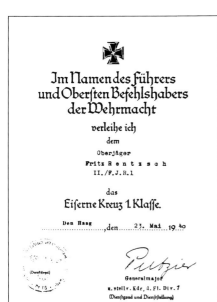

Im Namen des Führers
und Oberſten Befehlshabers
der Wehrmacht

verleihe ich

dem

Oberjäger

Fritz Rentzsch

II./F.J.R.1

das

Eiſerne Kreuz 1.Klaſſe.

Den Haag ,den 23. Mai 19 40

Generalmajor

u. ſtellv. Kdr. d. Fl. Div. 7

(Dienſtgrad und Dienſtſtellung)

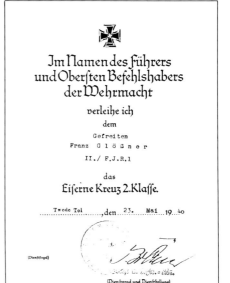

Im Namen des Führers
und Oberſten Befehlshabers
der Wehrmacht

verleihe ich

dem

Gefreiten

Franz Glößner

II./F.J.R.1

das

Eiſerne Kreuz 2.Klaſſe.

Twede Tol ,den 23. Mai 19 40

(Dienſtgrad und Dienſtſtellung)

Award document for the Iron Cross 1st Class. Note that it is signed by Generalmajor Putzier, who commanded the 7th Flying Division, as temporary replacement for General Student who was wounded in Holland.

Verleihungsurkunde zum Eisernen Kreuz, erster Klasse, unterzeichnet vom Generalmajor Putzier, zeitweilig Kommandeur der 7. Fliegerdivision in Vertretung für den verwundeten General Student.

Award document for the Iron Cross 2nd Class, signed by Oberst Bräuer, commander of Parachute Regiment 1.

Verleihungsurkunde zum Eisernen Kreuz, zweiter Klasse, unterzeichnet vom Oberst Bräuer, Kommandeur Fallschirmjägerregiment 1.

A wall painting in Brunswick, 6th Company.
Wandschmuck der 6. Kp. in Braunschweig.

Upon the successful completion of the campaign, the battalion was sent to The Haag and on June 1, returned to its home base. Immediately, new orders were received for the Narvik area in Norway and the battalion, now equipped with mountain clothing, arrived at the Norwegian airfield at Werns after a journey by rail and ship. General Dietl had stabilized the situation in Narvik by this time and the services of the battalion were not needed. They returned to their barracks again and at one time were slated for the abortive victory parade in Paris. When this event was cancelled, the unit returned to Germany via the battlefields of the First World War. At Verdun, the regimental commander, Colonel Bräuer, informed his men that they would be transferred from the regiment to act as cadre for a new airborne regiment, Parachute Regiment 3. The commander of this unit was to be Major Richard Heydrich who was promoted to colonel.

On July 29, an ailing Captain Prager took leave of his old battalion and it was sent to the training area in Bergen where it was to establish the new regiment.

Nach Ende der erfolgreichen Kämpfe um die Festung Holland ging es zunächst nach Den Haag, dann am 01.06.1940 zurück in den Friedensstandort. Kaum waren die stürmischen Siegesfeiern überstanden, kam ein neuer Auftrag: Einsatz im Raum Narvik. Dazu wurde das Bataillon mit Gebirgskleidung ausgerüstet und ab 05.06.1940 im Eisenbahn- u. Schiffstransport bis zu dem Absprungflugplatz Wernes bei Trondheim gebracht. Jedoch die günstige Lageentwicklung in Norwegen machte den Einsatz zur Unterstützung des deutschen Expeditionskorps unter General Dietl hinfällig. Kaum nach Braunschweig zurückgekehrt, erhielt das Bataillon wieder einen neuen, diesmal friedlichen Einsatzauftrag: Die Teilnahme an der Siegesparade in Paris. Doch die Parade entfiel aus politischen Gründen, und man genoss in der französischen Metropole den Urlaub.

Der Rückmarsch wurde u.a. dazu genutzt, um die alten Schlachtfelder des 1. Weltkrieges zu besuchen. Bei Verdun, wo der Rgt. Kdr. Fallschirmjäger-Regiment 1, Oberst Bräuer, selbst über ein Jahr den blutigen Grabenkrieg erlebt hatte, verabschiedete er die Soldaten seines II. Bataillons aus dem Regiment mit dem Auftrag, als Stammtruppe das neuaufzustellende Fallschirmjäger-Regiment 3 möglichst schnell einsatzbereit zu machen. Der neue Regimentskommandeur war allen alten Fallschirminfanteristen wohlbekannt: Major Richard Heidrich, inzwischen zum Oberst befördert. Am 29.07. verabschiedete sich Hauptmann Prager von seinem alten Bataillon. Dann ging es zum Truppübungsplatz Bergen zur Neuaufstellung des Fallschirmjäger-Regimentes 3.

New mountain uniforms for the paratroopers.
So sieht ein Fallschirmjäger in Gebirgsjägeruniform aus.

Below: Preparing for another mission: Narvik! Packing the containers.
Unten: Vorbereitung des II./FJR 1 für einen geplanten Sprungeinsatz in Narvik. Beladen der Sprungbehälter im Standort.

Via railroad to Denmark, and from there to Oslo by ship.
Abschiedsphoto in Deutschland. Jetzt geht es per Schiff weiter nach Norwegen.

Aalborg, Denmark.
Verladen in Aalborg, Dänemark.

Paratroopers on the way to Oslo as mountain troops, 6th Company.
Fallschirmjäger der 6. Kp. als Gebirgsjäger bei der Marine auf dem Weg nach Oslo.

Via railroad to Trondheim.
In Norwegen per Eisenbahn, teilweise durch das neutrale Schweden, in Richtung Trondheim.

Vaernes airfield. It was planned to carry the II./FJR 1 from here to Narvik and drop them there as reinforcements for General Dietl. But again, too late...Narvik was already a victory for the mountain troops.
Auf dem Fliegerhorst Vaernes. Von hier sollte es per Flugzeug zum Einsatzraum nach Narvik gehen. Doch die Gebirgsjäger hatten inzwischen gesiegt, der Einsatz des II./FJR 1 entfiel.

Vaernes airfield near Trondheim.
Der Flugplatz Vaernes bei Trondheim.

Paratroopers as ski troops - but without snow or skis!
Holmenkol, Norway.
Fallschirmjäger als Skispringer - zum Glück ohne Schnee und
Skier!

Unteroffizier Hagl, who later earned the Knight's Cross (with his comrades at Holmenkol).

Unteroffizier Hagl, der später mit dem Ritterkreuz ausgezeichnet wurde, mit seinen Kameraden an der Holmenkol-Sprungschanze.

Above: Hptm. Prager, Oberst Bräuer, Olt. v.d. Schulenburg, Hptm. Rau, Olt. Stangenberg (from left to right).

Oben: Hptm. Prager, Oberst Bräuer, Olt. v.d. Schulenburg, Hptm. Rau, Olt. Stangenberg (von links nach rechts).

Oslo: Unteroffizier H. Mordhorst wearing the cap of a mountain trooper.

Oslo: Unteroffizier H. Mordhorst mit Gebirgsjägermütze.

Via ship and railroad back to Germany.
Von Oslo zurück per Schiff und Bahn.

Paris: June 1940 - July 22, 1940

Paris: Juni 1940 - 22.07.1940

After returning from Norway the battalion received orders to go to Paris for the victory parade. Although Hitler later cancelled his parade order, the paratroopers visited Paris and the surrounding area, such as the November 11, 1918 memorial above. The Germans later blew up this memorial in Compiegne.

Ende Juni traf das II./FJR 1 in Braunschweig wieder ein. Am 06.07.1940 kam der Befehl zur Teilnahme an der Siegesparade in Paris. Wenngleich die Parade auch ausfiel, Paris und Umgebung wurde genossen. Erinnerungsphoto am Mahnmal zur Kapitulation der Deutschen am 11. Nov. 1918, im Wald von Compiegne.

Paris could be visited only with a special visitor's permit. But many made the trip without it.
Mit Erlaubnisschein in Paris.

Grave of the Unknown Soldier in Paris.
Am Grab des unbekannten Soldaten.

Troopers Schulze and Hartmann, both without permits, are caught by Olt. Haedrich.

Ohne Erlaubnisschein! Erwischt wurden vom Olt. Haedrich die Fallschirmjäger Schulze und Hartmann.

Eine RM - **20** fr. N⁰ 43

STRAFE

für eine Übertretung im abgekürzten Verfahren.

AMENDE

p... non observation des règlements de circulation (immédiatement exigible).

Der Militärbefehlshaber in Frankreich

The consequence - a fine of 20 Reichsmarks!
Die Folge der Überschreitung: eine Strafe von 20 Reichsmark!

Visiting the Versailles castle.
Besuch des Schlosses von Versailles.

221

Good living in Paris ... with a permit!
So kann man mit Erlaubnisschein in Paris gut leben!

On its way home, on July 22, 1940, the battalion
turned off and visited Verdun and Fort Douamont.
Ab 22.07.1940 geht es von Paris zurück,
zunächst nach Verdun zum Fort Douamont.

Fort Douamont, 1940.

In Verdun the IInd Battalion is told it will leave FJR 1 in order to build up FJR 3. Oberst Bräuer says farewell to his soldiers (above). During World War I Bräuer fought for more than a year in the Verdun sector.

In Verdun verlässt das II./FJR 1 das Regiment, um als Stammtruppe das neue Fallschirmjäger-Regiment 3 aufzustellen. Hier verabschiedet Oberst Bräuer seine Soldaten. Bräuer war selbst im I. Weltkrieg über ein Jahr vor Verdun eingesetzt.

The way of the Army Airborne Infantry Battalion and the II./FJR 1.
Der Weg des Fallschirminf.-Btl. und des II./FJR 1.

225

ESTABLISHMENT OF PARACHUTE REGIMENT 3

AUFSTELLUNG FALLSCHIRMJÄGERREGIMENT 3

After the stunning Wehrmacht victories in the west, there was no lack of volunteers for paratroop units. Even the world boxing champion, Max Schmeling, applied and was accepted by the new regiment and would later take part in the rigors of the Crete campaign.

Colonel Heydrich and his adjutant, 1st Lieutenant Heckel, attached great importance to realistic and innovative infantry training. "Ability-Comradeship-Esprit de Corps" was Heydrich's motto. During this specialized training, Heydrich was able to use his numerous skills and it was through his efforts that all the young officers became masters of their trade and he saw to it that army officers who attended the Luftwaffe jump school became familiar with the special circumstances related to airborne employment. All of the men of Parachute Regiment 3 were accomplished jumpers and many still wore the Army Parachute Badge.

Nach den glänzenden Siegen der Wehrmacht im Westen drängten sich viele Offiziere, Unteroffiziere und Mannschaften freiwillig zur Fallschirmtruppe. Durch ihre Siege in Eben Emael, Moerdijk und Rotterdam hatten sie viel Lob und Ehre gesammelt, so dass es an Freiwilligen nicht mangelte. Sogar der Boxweltmeister Max Schmeling meldete sich freiwillig und kam zum Fallschirmjäger-Regiment 3. Er sollte dort den Einsatz Kreta miterleben.

Der neue Regimentskommandeur, Oberst Heidrich, sowie sein Adjutant, Olt. Heckel, legten, wie bereits im Fallschirminfanterie-Bataillon, grössten Wert auf kriegsnahe, infanteristische und phantasievolle Ausbildung. "Können - Kameradschaft - Korpsgeist" - war das Motto! Sowohl im Standort als auch auf Truppenübungsplätzen wurde mit Hilfe der alten und im Gefecht bereits erfahrenen Fallschirminfanteristen geübt, geschossen und ausgebildet. Man besuchte Lehrgänge an der Fallschirmsprungschule, bei der Reichsbahn und Wehrmacht und schulte vor allem das junge Offizierkorps in Taktik und Befehlsgebung. Hier zeigte der Regimentskommandeur sein ganz besonderes Können. Ihm war es zu verdanken, dass bald alle Offiziere ihr Handwerk beherrschten und die Heeresoffiziere mit der besonderen Situation des Fallschirmsprungeinsatzes bestens vertraut waren. Natürlich waren alle

After nearly nine months of intensive training, the regiment was eager for action and on April 26, 1941, their wishes were fulfilled. The regiment was alerted to prepare for a mission in southern Europe, with the same uniforms, equipment and armament as issued for the abortive Narvik campaign.

Their target would be the island of Crete where they would gain the laurels they missed in Norway.

Soldaten des Fallschirmjägerregimentes 3 ausgebildete Springer und die alten Fallschirminfanteristen trugen, wie ihr Kommandeur, voller Stolz noch immer das alte Heeresfallschirmschützenabzeichen!

Nach knapp neun Monaten intensiver Ausbildung war das Regiment voll ausgebildet und voller Tatendrang. Dann kam am 26.04.1941 die Alarmierung: Das Regiment hatte sich für einen Einsatz im Süden Europas bereitzumachen. Dass ihr Einsatz auf Kreta erfolgen und dieser mit hohen Verlusten verbunden sein würde, ahnte im April 1941 noch niemand!

The commanders: At left is Oberst Heidrich, former commander of the Army Airborne Infantry Battalion, now commander of the new FJR 3. At right is Hptm. Prager, former commander of II./FJR 1.

Die Kommandeure: Links, Oberst R. Heidrich, ehemals Kommandeur des Fallschirminfanteriebataillons, nun Kommandeur des neuen FJR 3, noch in Heeresuniform. Rechts, Hptm. Prager, ehem. Kommandeur des II./FJR 1.

Many volunteers transferred from the army to the paratroopers. Left to right: Heidrich, Prager, Fehse, Heilmann and Reinsdorf.

Viele Freiwillige meldeten sich vom Heer zur Fallschirmtruppe. Von links nach rechts: Heidrich, Prager, Fehse, Heilmann, Reinsdorf.

Left: Prager, behind him Hptm. Schlottke. Right: Heidrich, behind him Hptm. Fehse.

Links: Prager, dahinter Hptm. Schlottke. Rechts: Heidrich, dahinter Hptm. Fehse.

The first parade.
Vorbeimarsch.

Hptm. Prager and his faithful adjutant, Olt. Haedrich, who was killed in action on Crete on May 20, 1941.
Hptm. Prager und sein treuer Adjutant, Olt. Haedrich, gefallen am 20.05.1941 auf Kreta.

Fallschirm-Jäger Rgt.

Fallschirm-Jäger Rgt. 3

Above: The FJR 3 sleeveband was authorized by the OKL but not officially produced and issued to the paratroopers. Many soldiers, therefore, removed the number "1" and had the number "3" embroidered onto the sleeveband. Others ordered new sleevebands from private tailors.

Oben: Der FJR 3 Ärmelstreifen, vom OKL zwar genehmigt, doch offiziell nicht an das Regiment ausgegeben. Viele Soldaten haben von ihrem alten Ärmelstreifen die Nummer 1 entfernt und sich die Nummer 3 hineinsticken lassen oder sich besondere anfertigen lassen.

The tactical symbol of FJR 3.
Das taktische Zeichen des FJR 3.

V.d. Heydte, Wolfenbüttel,
1940.

Below: The 5th Company, FJR 3.
Unten: Die 5. Kompanie, FJR 3.

The 9th Company with Olt. Heilmann.
Die 9. Kompanie mit Olt. Heilmann.

The 9th Company, November 10, 1940.
Marsch zur Ausbildung: Die 9. Kompanie am 10.11.1940.

Locomotive training in Berlin-Rehagen and Jüterbog. Paratroopers must be trained for all situations, including running a locomotive.

Lokomotivausbildung in Berlin-Rehagen und Jüterbog. Fallschirmjäger im FJR 3 müssen alles können: auch eine Lokomotive fahren!

Below: Paratroopers must also be able to handle a captured tank.
Auch mit erbeuteten Panzern müssen Fallschirmjäger umgehen können.

Jump training again.
Und immer wieder Fallschirmsprungdienst.

Der Reichsminister der Luftfahrt   Berlin,den 15.Januar 1941
und Oberbefehlshaber der Luftwaffe

                B e f ä h i g u n g s n a c h w e i s

Auf Grund der Teilnahme an einem Lehrgang vom 6.Jan. bis

15.Jan.1941 und des Prüfungsergebnisses vom 14. Januar 1941

wird dem

            Obj. F u n k e, Hubert

bestätigt, dass er zum

Prüfer für Sprungfallschirme für den Bereich der Luftwaffe

sehr gut geeignet ist.

Dieser Befähigungsnachweis berechtigt den Inhaber nicht zur

Prüfung von Rettungsfallschirmen.

                 Der Prüfungsausschuss:

                 JL Oberstabsingenieur

Der Ausbildungsleiter: Der Prüfungskommissar:
                                 I.A.

Flieger-Stabsingenieur   Oberstleutnant
u. Ausbildungsleiter
m. b. W. b. O. b.

Testimony for a rigger of a RZ-1.
Befähigungsnachweis zum Prüfer für Sprungfallschirme.

Hptm. Fritz Prager, former commander of II./FJR 1, died on December 3, 1940 after a painful and long illness. He was buried in Bautzen.
Hptm. Fritz Prager, Kommandeur II./FJR 1, starb am 03.12.1940 nach langer und schwerer Krankheit. Er wurde in Bautzen mit militärischen Ehren beigesetzt.

Bautzen - farewell from his fellow paratroopers.
Bautzen - Abschied von einem guten Kameraden!

All officers of the fledgling parachute troops took part in the funeral of Major Prager. He remains unforgotten within the ranks of the paratroopers.

Alle Offiziere der jungen Fallschirmtruppe nahmen Abschied von Major Prager. Er bleibt in den Reihen der Fallschirmjäger unvergessen.

Christmas 1940.
Weihnachten 1940.

Winter training.
Winterkampfausbildung in Braunschweig.

Schliersee. The 7th Company with HFw. Gramse (left) and platoon leader OFw. Allmendinger (right).
Am Schliersee. OFw. Allmendinger (rechts) meldet die auf Skiern angetretene 7. Kompanie dem HFw. Gramse (links).

The 8th Company learns to ski.

Auch die 8. Kompanie betrieb Skiausbildung.

Above: Grete Weiser and other movie stars visit the regiment.
Oben: Grete Weiser und andere Schauspieler zu Besuch.

Max Schmeling, former heavyweight boxing champion of the world.
Max Schmeling, ehemaliger Boxweltmeister.

Above: On their way to a shooting range and training area again, Bergen, March 1941.

Oben: Und wieder geht es zur Ausbildung, diesmal auf den Truppenübungsplatz Bergen, März 1941.

9th Company, March 1941.
Die 9. Kompanie auf dem Marsch.

Below: The 3rd Company, Fw. Heide's platoon.
Unten: Die 3. Kompanie, Zug Fw. Heide.

New tactical orders, 7th Company.
Befehlsausgabe bei der 7. Kompanie.

The Panzerbüchse 38.
Fallschirmjäger mit der Panzerbüchse 38.

Urkunde

Der   **Oberjäger**   **Wagner**

hat beim   **Nachrichten - Wettkampf**

des   / Fallschirm=Jäger=Rgt. 3

am   **25. Oktober 1940**

im   **Schlüsseln**

den **3.** Preis errungen

Oberst u. Rgt. Kdr.

244   Document for a cryptography championship within FJR 3.
Ehrenurkunde für einen Nachrichten-Wettkampf im FJR 3.

The 3rd Company in Bergen.
Die 3. Kompanie in Bergen.

The radio team of IInd Battalion, FJR 3.
Der Funktrupp des II. Btl. bei der Ausbildung.

Officers of FJR 3 in Wolfenbüttel, April 1941. Left to right: Veth, Foltin (?), Dr. Petritsch, Dr. Hass, Klein, ? , Knoche, Krüger, Straehler-Pohl, ?, Haedrich, Peiser, ? , Gehrke, ? , ? .

Offiziere des FJR 3 in Wolfenbüttel, April 1941. Von links nach rechts: Veth, Foltin (?), Dr. Petritsch, Dr. Hass, Klein, ? , Knoche, Krüger, Straehler-Pohl, ? , Haedrich, Peiser, ? , Gehrke, ? , ? .

A last portrait shortly before the new mission (Crete).

Ein letztes Foto vor dem neuen Einsatz (Kreta).

APPENDICES

ANLAGEN

1: Chronicle and Engagement Calendar of Assault Battalion, 2nd Army, and Assault Battalion No. 7

August 9, 1916 - Establishment of Assault Battalion, 2nd Army in Beuville.

August 26, 1916 - Order issued for establishment and location of the Assault Battalion in Etaves.

October 19, 1916 - Attack on La Maisonnette.

November 20, 1916 - Establishment of Assault Battalion No. 7 in Bosmont, Tavaux and Marle.

March 16-24, 1917 - First missions south of Ailles, Loivre, with the 25th Landwehr Division.

April 4, 1917 - Mission with the 10th Reserve Division at Sapigneul.

April 16, 1917 - Defensive battle at Arras and Prouvais.

April 25, 1917 - Attack at Hurtebise-Ferme with the 1st Guard Division, and with the 20th Infantry Division at Courtecon.

May 11, 1917 - Attack with the 11th Bavarian Infantry Division.

May 16, 1917 - Attack with the 211th Infantry Division at Laffaux-Vauxaillon.

May 25, 1917
June 1, 1917
June 6, 1917 } Attacks in the Pargny, Filain area.
June 20, 1917

July 8, 1917
July 14, 1917 } Attacks in the Pargny, Courtecon, Royere-Ferme areas.
August 10, 1917

June 3-31, 1917 - Battles at Chemin des Dames.

October 23, 1917 - Battle at Laffaux.

October 5, 1917
November 18, 1917
November 30, 1917 } Reconnaissance battles at Chevregny,
December 5, 1917 } Septvaux, Juvincourt.
December 9, 1917
December 13, 1917

January 5, 1918
February 3, 1918 } Reconnaissance battles and missions in
March 18, 1918 } the Juvincourt, Fresnes areas.

March-April 1918 - Missions as part of the "Great Battle in France" ("Michael").

May-June 1918 - Battle between Saissons and Reims.

July 15, 1918 - Attack on the Marne River.

July 18 - August 8, 1918 - Defensive battles in Soissons, Villers-Bretonneux.

November 9, 1918 - Last parade of Assault Battalion No. 7 in honor of the Army commander, Generaloberst von Boehn.

November-December 1918 - Missions in Marburg.

December 1918-January 1919 - Moving from Marburg to Kassel.

February 1919 - Assault Battalion No. 7 is deactivated.

After February 1919 - Established as the guard unit for the Army High Command (OHL) in Kolberg/Pomerania, and as "Freikorps Feldmarschall Hindenburg."

■

1: Chronik und Gefechtskalender
Sturmabteilung 2. Armee und Sturmbataillon Nr. 7

09.08.1916 - Beginn der Aufstellung Sturmabteilung 2. Armee in Beuville.

26.08.1916 - Aufstellungsbefehl und Stationierung in Etaves.

19.10.1916 - Angriff auf La Maisonnette.

20.11.1916 - Beginn Aufstellung Sturmbataillon Nr. 7 in Bosmont, Tavaux und Marle.

16.03-24.03.1917 - 1. Einsätze südl. Ailles, Loivre und bei 25. Landwehr-Division.

04.04.1917 - Einsatz bei 10. Res. Div., Sapigneul.

16.04.1917 - Abwehrschlacht bei Arras und Prouvais.

25.04.1917 - Angriff bei Hurtebise-Ferme, 1. Garde-Div. und bei Courtecon, 20. Inf. Div.

11.05.1917 - Angriff bei 11. Bayer. Inf. Div.

16.05.1917 - Angriff bei Laffaux-Vauxaillon, 211. Inf. Div.

25.05.1917
01.06.1917
06.06.1917 } Angriffe in den Raum Pargny, Filain.
20.06.1917

08.07.1917
14.07.1917 } Angriffe bei Pargny, Courtecon, Royere-Ferme.
10.08.1917

03.06-31.07.1917 - Kämpfe am Chemin des Dames.

23.10.1917 - Schlacht bei Laffaux.

05.10.1917	
18.11.1917	
30.11.1917	Gewaltsame Erkundungen bei Chevregny,
05.12.1917	Septvaux, Juvincourt.
09.12.1917	
13.12.1917	

05.01.1918	Gewaltsame Erkundungen und Einsätze bei
03.02.1918	Juvincourt, Fresnes.
18.03.1918	

März/April 1918 - Teilnahme an der "Grossen Schlacht in Frankreich" ("Michael").

Mai/Juni 1918 - Schlacht zwischen Soissons und Reims.

15.07.1918 - Angriffsschlacht an der Marne.

18.07-08.08.1918 - Abwehrkämpfe Soissons, Villers-Bretonneux.

09.11.1918 - Letztes geschlossenes Antreten des Sturmbataillon Nr. 7 vor dem Armeeführer, Generaloberst von Boehn.

Nov./Dez. 1918 - Einsatz in Marburg.

Dez. 1918/Jan. 1919 - Verlegung nach Kassel.

Febr. 1919 - Demobilisierung Sturmbataillon Nr. 7.

ab Febr. 1919 - Aufstellung Wachkommando OHL in Kolberg/Pommern und "Freikorps Feldmarschall Hindenburg."

2: Chronicle and Engagement Calendar of the Airborne Infantry and II./FJR 1

April 1, 1937 - Establishment of the Airborne Infantry Company.

May 4-June 6, 1937 - First jump course of the Airborne Infantry Company at Stendal.

August 20/September 20, 1937 - Two fatal jump accidents.

Autumn 1937 - Major R. Heidrich is commander of the company.

November/December 1937 - Major Heidrich's jump course.

Spring 1938 - Company participation in the naval maneuver and jump on Borkum.

June 1, 1938 - Expansion to battalion strength (Abn.Inf.Bn.).

October 7-17, 1938 - First Sudentenland mission.

November 4, 1938 - Moving from Stendal to Braunschweig, getting the infantry standard and the traditions of Assault Battalion No. 7.

January 1, 1939 - Transferring from the army to the air force (Luftwaffe) as the II. Battalion/Parachute Regiment 1. Hptm. Prager is the first battalion commander.

March 14-20, 1939 - Second Sudetenland mission in Prague.

April 20 and June 20, 1939 - Parades in Berlin.

July 5-12, 1939 - Live-shooting training at Hammerstein.

August 2-15, 1939 - Live-shooting and training at Wildflecken.

September 1939 - Polish campaign.

September 20-24, 1939 - First combat mission at Iwangerod-Ulenz-Wola Gulowka.

May 2, 1940 - Getting orders for the Holland campaign, moving to Werl.

May 9, 1940 - Receiving the code-word for Holland.

May 10, 1940 - The first wave takes off at 0450 hours.

May 12, 1940 - First contact with the 9th Panzer Division.

May 21, 1940 - Marching into The Haag.

June 1, 1940 - Return to Braunschweig.

June 3-4, 1940 - Preparation for the Narvik mission.

June 5, 1940 - March to Oslo.

June 17, 1940 - Return to Braunschweig.

July 6, 1940 - March to Paris, via Eben Emael and Versailles.

July 22, 1940 - IInd Battalion transferred out of FJR 1 in Verdun by Oberst Bräuer, and then returned to Braunschweig.

July 30, 1940 - Arrival in Bergen.

August 1, 1940 - Beginning the establishment of FJR 3, with Oberst R. Heidrich as its first commander.

October 1940 - Participation in a movie on the Holland campaign by Tobis-Topical.

December 3, 1940 - Death of Major Prager, military funeral in Bautzen.

---

2. Chronik und Gefechtskalender der Fallschirm-Infanterie und des II./FJR 1

01.04.1937 - Aufstellung der Fallschirminfanterie-Kompanie (F.I.K.).

04.05.-03.06.1937 - 1. Springerlehrgang der F.I.K.

20.08./20.09.1937 - Tödliche Sprungunfälle.

Herbst 1937 - Major Heidrich übernimmt die F.I.K.

Nov./Dez. 1937 - Springerlehrgang Maj. Heidrich.

Frühjahr 1938 - Teilnahme der F.I.K. am Flottenmanöver.

ab 01.06.1938 - Aufstellung und Erweiterung der F.I.K. zum Fallschirminfanterie-Bataillon (F.I.B.).

07.10.-17.10.1938 - Teilnahme am Sudeteneinsatz.

04.11.1938 - Einmarsch in den neuen Friedensstandort Braunschweig, Übernahme der Truppenfahne und der Tradition des Sturmbataillon Nr. 7.

ab 01.01.1939 - Übernahme des F.I.B. als II. Btl., Fallschirmjäger-Regiment 1 der Luftwaffe. Hptm. Prager wird Bataillonskommandeur.

14.03.-20.03.1939 - Besetzung Prag.

20.04./20.06.1939 - Paraden in Berlin.

05.-12.07.1939 - Truppenübungsplatzaufenthalt Hammerstein.

02.-15.08.1939 - Truppenübungsplatzaufenthalt Wildflecken.

September 1939 - Polenfeldzug.

20.-24.09.1939 - Einsätze im Raum Iwangerod-Ulenz-Wola Gulowka.

02.05.1940 - Eintreffen Verlegebefehl zum Absprungflugplatz Werl.

09.05.1940 - Eingang Stichwort für den Holland-Einsatz.

10.05.1940 - Start der 1. Welle um 0450 Uhr.

12.05.1940 - Erste Verbindung zur 9. Pz.Div.

21.05.1940 - Einmarsch in Den Haag.

ab 01.06.1940 - Rückmarsch in den Friedensstandort.

03.-04.06.1940 - Vorbereitungen zum Narvik-Einsatz.

ab 05.06.1940 - Marsch nach Oslo.

17.06.1940 - Rückmarsch nach Braunschweig.

06.07.1940 - Fahrt nach Frankreich über Eben Emael-Versailles nach Paris. 251

22.07.1940 - Rückmarsch in den Standort. Verabschiedung des II./FJR 1 aus dem Bereich des Fallschirmjäger-Regiment 1 durch Oberst Bräuer in Verdun.

30.07.1940 - Eintreffen auf dem Truppenübungsplatz Bergen.

ab 01.08.1940 - Beginn der Aufstellung des Fallschirmjäger-Regiment 3, Kommandeur: Oberst Richard Heidrich.

Oktober 1940 - Teilnahme an den Filmaufnahmen "Hollandeinsatz" für die TOBIS-Wochenschau.

03.12.1940 - Tod Major Prager, militärische Beisetzung in Bautzen.

3: The Knight's Cross Holders of II./FJR 1

3: Die Ritterkreuzträger des II./FJR 1

Fritz Prager
Born in Wolfenbüttel, December 17, 1905.

November 26, 1930 - Joined the Reichswehr, Inf. Rgt. 10.

June 1, 1938 - Commander of MG-company, Airborne Infantry Battalion.

January 1, 1939 - Commander of II./FJR 1.

September 1939 - Campaign in Poland.

October 13, 1939 - Received the Iron Cross, 2nd Class.

May 10, 1940 - Moerdijk mission, where he was badly wounded.

June 19, 1940 - Promotion to Major.

July 1, 1940 - Commander of II./FJR 3.

December 3, 1940 - Major Prager died after a long illness. He was buried in Bautzen.

Knight's Cross (No. 37) - May 24, 1940.
Last rank: - Major

Fritz Prager
Geboren am 17.12.1905 in Wolfenbüttel.

26.11.1930 - Eintritt in die Reichswehr beim Infanterie-Regiment 10.

ab 01.06.1938 - Chef MG-Kompanie im Fallschirminfanterie-Bataillon.

ab 01.01.1939 - Kommandeur II./Fallschirmjäger-Regiment 1.

September 1939 - Polenfeldzug.

13.10.1939 - Verleihung Eisernes Kreuz II. Klasse.

10.05.1940 - Sprungeinsatz bei Moerdijk, dabei schwere Verwundung.

ab 19.06.1940 - Major.

ab 01.07.1940 - Kommandeur II./Fallschirmjäger-Regiment 3.

03.12.1940 - Major Prager verstarb nach langer Krankheit in Frankfurt. Beerdigung in Bautzen.

Ritterkreuz (37) am 24.05.1940.
Letzter Dienstgrad: Major.

Fritz
Prager.

Karl Alfred Schwarzmann
Born in Fürth, March 23, 1912.

April 1, 1933 - Entered the Reichswehr, 13th Co., Inf. Rgt. 21, Nuremberg.

August 1936 - Participant in the XIth Olympic Games in Berlin, where he won the gold medal three times and the bronze medal twice.

June 30, 1938 - Left the army and became an army sports teacher at the Army Sports School in Wünsdorf.

January 1, 1939 - Entered the II./FJR 1 (reactivation).

April 1, 1939 - Leader of the MG-platoon, 8th Company, II./FJR 1.

September 1939 - Campaign in Poland.

May 10, 1940 - Moerdijk mission, where he was badly wounded.

June 8, 1940 - Transferred as a reserve officer from the army to the air force/paratroops.

May 1941 - Crete campaign.

Winter 1941/42 - First missions in Russia.

June 27, 1942 - Leader of the 8th Company, II./FJR 3.

October 15, 1942 - Commander of the 8th Company

1942/43 - Second missions in Russia.

June 15, 1943 - Commander of the Staff Quarters, 7th Flying Division/1st Abn. Div.

May 9-October 29, 1945 - British prisoner of war.

Knight's Cross (No. 45) - May 29, 1940 as 1st. Lieutenant (Res.) and MG-platoon leader, 8th Co., II./FJR 1.
Last rank: Major (Res.).

Karl Alfred Schwarzmann
Geboren am 23.03.1912 in Fürth.

01.04.1933 - Eintritt als Freiwilliger in die 13. Kompanie Infanterie-Regiment 21 (Nürnberg).

August 1936 - Teilnahme an den XI. Olympischen Spielen 1936 in Berlin. Dreifacher Goldmedaillengewinner und zweifacher Bronzemedaillengewinner im Mannschafts- und Einzelturnen.

ab 01.01.1939 - Verwendung im II./Fallschirmjäger-Regiment 1.

ab 01.04.1939 - MG-Zugführer in der 8. Kompanie II./FJR 1.

September 1939 - Polenfeldzug.

10.05.1940 - Sprungeinsatz Moerdijk, dabei schwere Verwundung als Zugführer in der 8. Kompanie.

ab 08.06.1940 - Wechsel als Res. Offz. des Heeres zur Luftwaffe als Res. Offz. (Fallschirmtruppe).

Mai 1941 - Einsatz mit der Seestaffel auf Kreta.

Winter 1941/42 - 1. Russlandeinsatz.

ab 27.06.1942 - Führer 8. Kompanie, II./Fallschirmjäger-Regiment 3.

ab 15.10.1942 - Kompaniechef 8. Kompanie, II./FJR 3.

1942/43 - 2. Russlandeinsatz.

ab 15.06.1943 - Kommandant Stabsquartier 7. Fliegerdivision bzw. 1. Fallschirmjäger-Division.

09.05.-29.10.1945 - Britische Kriegsgefangenschaft.

Ritterkreuz (45) am 29.05.1940 als Oberleutnant d. Reserve und MG-Zugführer 8. Kompanie, II./FJR 1.

Letzter Dienstgrad: Major d. Res.

Karl Alfred
Schwarzmann.

Cord Hermann Johann Tietjen
Born in Danzig, November 10, 1914.

October 20, 1936 - Entered the Wehrmacht, 2nd Company, Eng. Bn. 20, Hamburg.

October 9, 1937 - Transferred to the Army Airborne Infantry Company.

December 1937 - Jump course.

June 1, 1938 - Eng. platoon, Army Abn. Inf. Bn.

January 28, 1939 - Platoon leader, 5th Company, II./FJR 1.

September 1939 - Campaign in Poland.

May 10, 1940 - Moerdijk mission, where he succeeded in taking the road bridge by knocking-out the defensive bunkers.

August 2, 1940 - Transferred to Abn. Eng. Bn. 7 (7th Flying Division).

September 1, 1940 - Commander of the 1st. Company, Abn. Eng. Bn. 7.

May 20, 1941 - Crete campaign with the Abn. Eng. Bn. 7, attached to FJR 3.

February 21, 1942 - Commander of 2nd. Company/Corps Abn. Eng. Bn. (Major Witzig).

1942 - North African campaign with Brigade Ramcke.

November 5, 1942 - Prisoner of war.

Knight's Cross (No. 46) - May 24, 1940.
Last rank: Hauptmann (Captain).

Cord Hermann Johann Tietjen
Geboren 10.11.1914 in Danzig.

20.10.1936 - Eintritt als Freiwilliger in die Wehrmacht, 2. Kp. Pionierbataillon 20, Hamburg.

09.10.1937 - Versetzung zur Fallschirminfanterie-Kompanie (F.I.K.).

Dezember 1937 - Fallschirmsprungausbildung.

ab 01.06.1938 - Verwendung im Pionierzug Fallschirminfanterie-Bataillon (F.I.B.), Teilnahme Besetzung Sudetenland.

ab 28.01.1939 - Zugführer in der 5. Kp. II./Fallschirmjäger-Regiment 1

September 1939 - Teilnahme am Polenfeldzug.

10.05.1940 - Sprungeinsatz in Holland, Moerdijk, dort entscheidender Einsatz als Zugführer in der 5. Kp. und Eroberung der Strassenbrücke.

ab 02.08.1940 - Versetzung zum Fallschirmpionier-Bataillon 7 (7. Fliegerdivision).

ab 01.09.1940 - Kompaniechef 1. Kp./Fsch.Pi.Btl. 7.

ab 20.05.1941 - Kreta-Einsatz mit Fsch.Pi.Btl. 7 im Rahmen der Kampfgruppe Heidrich.

ab 21.02.1942 - Kompaniechef 2. Kp./Korps-Fallschirmpionier-Bataillon (Major Witzig).

1942 - Einsatz in Afrika im Rahmen der Brigade Ramcke.

05.11.1942 - Britische Gefangenschaft.

Ritterkreuz (46) am 24.05.1940.
Letzter Dienstgrad: Hauptmann ab 01.03.1943.

Cord Hermann Johann Tietjen.

Vorläufiges Besitzzeugnis

Der Führer
und Oberste Befehlshaber
der Wehrmacht

hat

dem Leutnant Cord T i e t j e n

das Ritterkreuz
des Eisernen Kreuzes

am 24. Mai 1940 verliehen.

Hauptquartier d.Ob.d.L. , den 25. Juni 1940

Der Chef des Luftwaffenpersonalamts

Generalleutnant

Knight's Cross Holders/Former Members of Army Abn.Inf. Company/Battalion

Ritterkreuzträger, die im FiK/FiB oder II./FJR 1 dienten

Rudolf Witzig

Born in Röhlinghausen, Westfalia, on August 14, 1916.

April 1, 1935 - Officer candidate in Eng. Bn. 16, Höxter.

August 1, 1938 - Eng. platoon, Army Airborne Infantry Battalion.

October 30, 1939 - Commander of Eng. platoon, Fallschirmjäger-Sturmabteilung Koch.

May 10, 1940 - Eben-Emael mission.

August 1, 1940 - Commander of 9th Company, Fallschirmjäger-Sturmregiment.

May 1941 - Crete mission.

May 10, 1942 - Corps Abn. Eng. Bn.

May 1, 1944 - Commander of I./Abn. Eng. Rgt. 21.

December 16, 1944 - Commander of FJR 18.

May 8-September 17, 1945 - Prisoner of war.

Knight's Cross (No. 16) - May 10, 1940.
Oak Leaves (No. 662) - November 25, 1944.

Rudolf Witzig

Geboren am 14.08.1916 in Röhlinghausen, Westf.

01.04.1935 - Fahnenjunker im Pionierbataillon 16, Höxter.

01.08.1938 - Pionierzug F.i.B.

30.10.1939 - Führer Pionierzug, Fallschirmjäger-Sturmabt. Koch.

10.05.1940 - Einsatz gegen die belg. Festung Eben Emael.

01.08.1940 - Kp. Chef 9. Kp. Fsch.Jg.Sturm-Rgt.

Mai 1941 - Kreta-Einsatz.

10.05.1942 - Korps Fallschirm-Pionierbataillon.

01.05.1944 - Kommandeur I./Fsch.Pi.Rgt. 21.

16.12.1944 - Kommandeur Fsch.Jg.Rgt. 18.

08.05.-17.09.1945 - Kriegsgefangenschaft.

Ritterkreuz (16) am 10.05.1940.
Eichenlaub (662) am 25.11.1944.

Rudolf
Witzig.

Below: Witzig and Gritzbach, an adjutant to
Göring.
Unten: Witzig und Gritzbach, Adjutant bei
Göring.

Vorläufiges Besitzeugnis

Der Führer
und Oberste Befehlshaber
der Wehrmacht

hat

dem Oberleutnant Rudolf W i t z i g

das Ritterkreuz
des Eisernen Kreuzes

am 10. Mai 1940 verliehen.

Hauptquartier d.Ob.d.L. **den** 25. Juni 1940
Der Chef des Luftwaffenpersonalamts

Generalleutnant

4a: Organization of a Parachute Regiment.

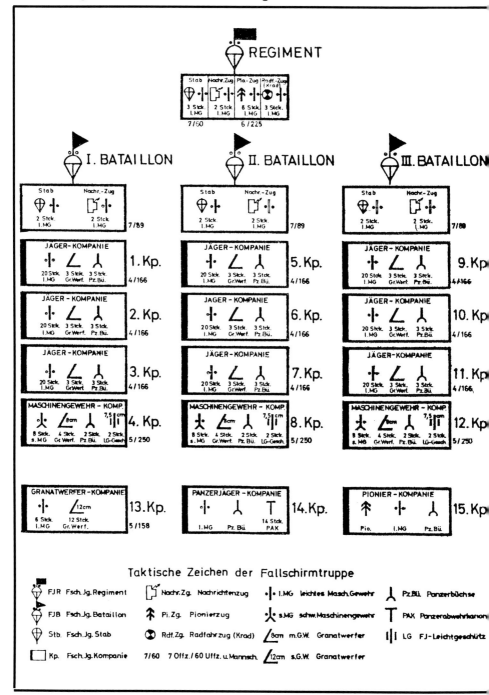

4a: Gliederung eines Fallschirmjägerregimentes.

4b: Weapons of a Parachute Regiment.

Waffenbild	Kurz-bezeichnung	Beschreibung und technische Daten
P 38 Eierhandgranate Stielhandgranate	P 08 P 38 St. Hd.Gr. Eier-Hd.Gr.	PISTOLE 08: Kaliber 9 mm; Gewicht 915 g; Magazin 8 Schuß; Rückstoßlader mit Kniehebelverschluß und beweglichem Lauf. PISTOLE 38: Kaliber 9 mm; Gewicht 865 g; Magazin 8 Schuß; Fabrikat "Walther". STIELHANDGRANATE 24: Gewicht 1 kg; Sprengladung 200 Gramm; Brennzeit 4,5 Sekunden. EIERHANDGRANATE: Brennzeit 4 Sekunden.
MP 40	MP 40	MASCHINENPISTOLE 38/40: Für Nahkampf, Wald- und Ortsgefechte. Rückstoßlader für 9 mm Pistolenpatronen, wie bei der 08 u. P 38; Stangenmagazin 32 Schuß; Waffenlänge 62/86 cm; Gewicht 4,3 kg; Feuerstöße von 5 - 10 Schuß; beste Schußweite bis 100 m, größte Weite 200 m.
Karabiner 98 k Sturmgewehr 44	98 k FJ-G 42 Gw. Gr.	KARABINER 98 k: Waffe für gezielten Einzelschuß; Kaliber 7,9 mm; Länge 1,11 m; Gewicht 3,9 kg; Ladestreifen mit 5 Patronen. FALLSCHIRMJÄGERGEWEHR 42: Kaliber 7,9 mm, normale Inf.-Munition; Waffenlänge 93 cm; Gewicht 4,6 kg; abnehmbares Kastenmagazin; Einzel- und Dauerfeuer: Gesamtherstellung 5000 Stück. GEWEHRGRANATE: Sprenggranate für Flach- und Steilfeuer; auch als Handgranate verwendbar; auf Karabiner und Sturmgewehr aufsetzbar; Reichweite bis 500 m; 40 mm Panzerdurchschlag auf 50 m.
	St.Gw.44	STURMGEWEHR 44: Feuerkräftige Waffe für Einzelkämpfer. Kaliber 7,9 mm, jedoch als Kurzpatrone; Waffenlänge 94 cm; Gewicht 5,4 kg; Magazin 32 Schuß; Reichweite 800 m; Einzelfeuer 30 - 50 Schuß/min bis 600 m; Dauerfeuer 60 - 90 Schuß/min bis 300 m.
l. MG 42 l. MG 34	l.MG 34 l.MG 42	MASCHINENGEWEHR 34: Kaliber 7,9 mm; wie beim Karabiner; Gewicht 11,5 kg; Reichweite 2000 m, max. 3500 m; Einzel- und Dauerfeuer; 15 Schuß/s = 900 Schuß/min; Patronenkasten mit 300 Schuß in 6 Gurtteilen oder 250 Schuß in einem Gurt. MASCHINENGEWEHR 42: Kaliber 7,9 mm; Waffenlänge 1,22 m; Gewicht 11,6 kg; Munitionszuführung wie beim MG 34; 25 Schuß/s ≈ 1500 Schuß/min. Feuerkraft, Bedienungs- und Hemmungssicherheit waren unübertroffen; auch "Elektrisches MG" oder "Knochensäge" genannt.
s.MG 34	s.MG 34 s.MG 42	Die Maschinengewehre waren Träger des Feuerkampfes im Angriff und als Sperrwaffe mit großer Wirkung in der Verteidigung. SCHWERES MASCHINENGEWEHR 34: Wie l.MG 34, jedoch mit MG-Lafette und Zieleinrichtung; Gewicht ca. 32 kg; Reichweite wie l. MG 34. SCHWERES MASCHINENGEWEHR 42: Wie l. MG 42, jedoch mit MG-Lafette und Zieleinrichtung; Gewicht ca. 32 kg; Reichweite wie l. MG 42.
m.GtWerf. 8cm	l. Gr.W. m.Gr. W. s. Gr. W.	Fallschirmjäger- und Infanteriebegleitwaffe; Steilfeuerwaffe. LEICHTER GRANATWERFER: Kaliber 5 cm; Rohrlänge 46,5 cm; Gewicht 14 kg; Wurfgranate 0,835 kg; Schußweite 50 - 450 m, max. 520 m. MITTLERER GRANATWERFER: Kaliber 8 cm; Rohrlänge 1,14 m; Gewicht 56,7 kg, dreiteilig; Wurfgranate 3,5 kg; Schußweite 60 - 1900 m, max. 2400 m; 12 Schuß/min; Splitterwirkung bis 50 m. SCHWERER GRANATWERFER: Kaliber 12 cm; Rohrlänge 1,85 m; Gewicht 282 kg; Wurfgranate 15,8 kg; Schußweite 400 - 6000 m.
s. Pz.Bü. 41 2,8cm	s.Pz.Bü. "Ofenrohr" "Pz.Faust"	SCHWERE PANZERBÜCHSE 41: Kaliber 2,8 cm; Rohrlänge 1,715 m; Gewicht 229 kg; Durchschlagleistung 55 mm Panzerung auf 400 m. PANZERSCHRECK "Ofenrohr": Kaliber 8,8 cm; Rohrlänge 1,70 m; sichere Zielweite 100 m; Reichweite 400 m; 2 Mann-Bedienung. PANZERFAUST: Rohr-∅ 5 cm; Länge 1,03 m; Gewicht 6,1 kg; beste Schußweite 25 - 50 m, max. 80 m; Durchschlag 200 mm Panzerung; diese Waffe durchschlug alle damals eingesetzten gegner.Panzer.
PAK 7,5 cm	3,7 PAK 4,2 PAK 5,0 PAK 7,5 PAK	3,7 cm-PANZERABWEHRKANONE: Kaliber 3,7 cm; Rohrlänge 1,665 m; Gewicht 450 kg; 10 - 15 Schuß/min; 65 mm Panzerung auf 100 m. 4,2 cm-PANZERABWEHRKANONE: Kaliber 4,2 cm; Rohrlänge 2,25 m; Gewicht 560 kg; 10 - 12 Schuß/min. 5 cm-PANZERABWEHRKANONE: Kaliber 5 cm; Rohrlänge 3,45 m; Gewicht 986 kg; 12 - 14 Schuß/min; 65/120 mm Panzerung auf 100 m. 7,5 cm-PANZERABWEHRKANONE: Kaliber 7,5 cm; Rohrlänge 3,45 m; Gewicht 1425 kg; 12 - 14 Schuß/min; 95/130 mm Panzerung auf 1000 m.
LG 2 10,5cm	LG 1 LG 2	Als Artilleriegeschütz vornehmlich für die Fsch.Truppe entwickelt. FALLSCHIRM-LEICHTGESCHÜTZ LG 1 (LG 40): Kaliber 7,5 cm; Rohrlänge 1,15 m; Gewicht 145 kg; Geschoß 6,5 kg; 12 Schuß/min; Reichweite 6800 m; Zugmittel Kettenkrad oder 2 Mann. FALLSCHIRM-LEICHTGESCHÜTZ LG 2 (LG 42): Kaliber 10,5 cm; Rohrlänge 1,38 m; Gewicht 385 kg; Geschoß 14,8 kg; 12 Schuß/min; Reichweite 7900 m; Zugmittel Kettenkrad oder 2 - 3 Mann; Kampfentfernung für Panzerabwehr 1500 m.

4b: Waffen eines Fallschirmjägerregimentes.

BIBLIOGRAPHY

BIBLIOGRAPHIE

Books/Bücher

Beekmann, Kurowski. "Der Kampf um die Festung Holland" (Verlag Mittler u. Sohn, Herford, 1981).

Böhmler, Haupt. "Fallschirmjäger" (Podzun Verlag, Bad Nauheim, 1961; Dorheim, 1971 (2. Auflage)).

Busch, E. "Die Fallschirmjäger-Chronik 1935-1945" (Podzun-Pallas-Verlag, 1983).

Dollinger, Hans. "Der Erste Weltkrieg in Bildern und Dokumenten" (Verlag Kurt Desch, München, 1965).

Gericke, W. "Hurra wir Springen" (K. Motz u. Co., Schongau, o.J.).

Götzel, H. "Generaloberst Kurt Student und seine Fallschirmjäger" (Podzun-Pallas-Verlag, Friedberg, 1980).

Gratz, Herbert. "Kamerad Fallschirm" (Verlag v. Carl Gerold's Sohn, Wien und Leipzig, 1937).

Herzfeld, Hans. "Der Erste Weltkrieg" (Editions Rencontre, Lausanne, 1969).

Merglen, A. "Geschichte und Zukunft der Luftlandetruppen" (Verlag Rombach, Freiburg, 1970).

Ristow, Fritz. "Sturmgrenadiere - Chronik des Sturmbataillon Nr. 7" (Stein-Verlag, Bonn Mannheim, 1959).

v. Roon. "Die Bildchronik der Fallschirmtruppe 1935-1945" (Podzun-Pallas-Verlag, 1985).

Schüttel. "Fallschirmtruppen und Luftinfanterie" (Verlag Mittler u. Sohn, Berlin, 1938).

Thomas, F./Wegmann, G. "Die Ritterkreuzträger der Deutschen Wehrmacht 1939-1945, Teil II: Fallschirmjäger" (Biblio-Verlag, Osnabrück, 1986).

Reports, Magazines, Manuscripts, Manuals

Zeitschriften, Berichte, Manuskripte, Vorschriften

Gefechtsbericht II./FJR 1, Kdr. vom 27.09.1939.

Gefechtsbericht II./FJR 1, 1a, v. 30.05.1940.

L.Dv. 1601 (E), Ausgabe 1940. Die Fallschirmgrundausbildung für die Fallschirmtruppe.

"Der Deutsche Fallschirmjäger," Heft Nr. 11-1952, 5-1953, 2-1959, 6-1962, 11-1972, 1-1977, 4-1978, 3-1979.

Trad. Gemeinschaft FschJgRgt 3 und ehem. FschInf, 17./18.06.1972

Heidrich, R. "Vom unsichtbaren Königreich der Deutschen," Manuskript 1945-1947.